BLUE ÖYSTER CULT

A Visual Biography

Martin Popoff

BLUE ÖYSTER CULT

A Visual Biography

Martin Popoff

WYMER
PUBLISHING
Bedford, England

First published in Great Britain in 2020
by Wymer Publishing
www.wymerpublishing.co.uk
Tel: 01234 326691
Wymer Publishing is a trading name of Wymer (UK) Ltd.

Copyright © 2024 Wymer Publishing

ISBN: 978-1-915246-47-9

The Author hereby asserts his rights to be identified
as the author of this work in accordance with sections
77 to 78 of the Copyright, Designs & Patents Act 1988.

All rights reserved. No part of this publication may be
reproduced or transmitted in any form or by any means,
electronic or mechanical, including photocopying, or any
information storage and retrieval system, without written
permission from the publisher.

This publication is sold subject to the condition that it shall not,
by way of trade or otherwise, be lent, re-sold, hired out or
otherwise circulated without the publishers prior consent in any
form of binding or cover other than that in which it is published
and without a similar condition including this condition
being imposed on the subsequent purchaser.

Every effort has been made to trace the copyright holders of the
photographs in this book but some were unreachable. We would
be grateful if the photographers concerned would contact us.

Typeset and Design by Andy Bishop/Tusseheia Creative
Printed by Halstan Printing Group

A catalogue record for this book is available from the British Library.

ROLL OF HONOUR

Wymer Publishing duly acknowledges the following people who all put their faith in this publication by pre-ordering it:

Mario Alexandre Abud	Ted Jones	Debbie Smith
Desmond Ambrose	Toben Junas	Lasse Sonne
Frank Basting	Jake Kamp	Mark Stears
Shane W. Bench	Pavel Kaňák	Tony Stevens
Philip, Celia & Ruth Birtwistle	Arno Kolster	Marc Stitsel
Ken Bjelke	Taylor Kurtz	Scott Stratton
Simon Blows	Todd Ladner	Danny Street
Alfred Bonhomme	Philippe La Vigne	Martin Stupka
Troy Bratland	William Legrand	Graham Tait
In honour of Adam and Brad Brown	Allan Lewis	Matt Thompson
Derek Busby	Andrea Manente	Matthew Trautwein
Joel Canonico	Makis Gerasimos Mavrogiannis	John Gardner Trimble
John Carey	Stephen McNary	Toshiaki Uekami
Diego Cattaneo	Kristin Esposito McRae	Wolfgang Uka
Del Clayman	Adam Morice	Eddy Vermeiren
Chris Cockrill	Melne Murphy	Kevin Walkley
Scott Corning	Andy Newman	Graham Whitelaw
Spencer Crispe	Wendy Newman	Thomas Wikgren
Richard Ellis	Michael Nix	Damien Wilker
Garry Fay	Carl Noonan	Emily Wilson
John Frontuto	Terrence O'Donnell	Nicholas Zinn
Alice Ghidoni	Gregory Orr	
Tony Gillard	Dave Packard	
Samuel Giove	Ronald Petersen	
Jim Glass	Cheryl Peterson	
Jason Gool	Dave Pritchard	
Gerard Guero	Philip Putman	
Peter Hannath	James Raffell	
Jeanette Hellwert	Rob Reich	
Callum Henderson	Patrick Rema	
Jacob Herkins	Tony Roberts	
Gerard Hill	Steven P Robinson	
Geoff Hufford	Courtney Rogers	
Anthony Huso	Ross Sampson	
Ib Jensen	Adam Savje	
Ross Jones	Rick Sisson	

CONTENTS

Introduction — 9

Origins Through the 1970s — 13

The 1980s — 91

The 1990s — 139

The 2000s Through 2024 — 153

Acknowledgements/Bibliography — 238

About The Author — 240

Introduction

Welcome one and all to this feast for the eyes but not so much words this time. I say *this* time, because as many of you know, myself and the good publisher of this book, Wymer Publishing have to our names a little something called *Agents of Fortune: The Blue Öyster Cult Story* that I must say has always been one of the band biographies I've done that is most near and dear to my heart. Why? Well, first off, BÖC are definitely one of my favourite bands, and additionally a band I play over and over again throughout the decades without fatigue. But more so, there are just so many damn interesting stories about that band's songs, mostly due to the army of lyric-writers that have contributed to the cause.

So for me — and hopefully for you as well — that book is the place to satisfy your Cult o' Curiosity in terms of the story of the band. But the trade paperback format was always going to be a little frustrating and limiting in terms of what we could present with respect to the band's visuals. That has been salved, sated and lubricated by *Blue Öyster Cult: A Visual Biography*, where, for the first time, all of us have been able to experience this highly visual band in book form through the glory of full colour, heavy metal, the red and the black, the black and silver.

But lest you not be piqued by pretty pictures alone, we haven't abdicated with respect to the story. I vowed to the bold Wymer brass that I wouldn't overlap in the least with the action-packed *Agents of Fortune* book, so when approached to sculpt the text for this one, I was adamant, first off, not to quote the band. Mission accomplished — let the five-guitar army's pantsuits speak for themselves. But, as many of you know, I'm a crazy man for the timeline books, having done probably twenty of those, so for your entertainment pleasure, I took it upon myself to come up with a detailed chronology of the band, and then give myself the luxury of saying my piece within the introductions that start of each of the decade's pictorial offerings.

A happy surprise was discovering how much extra hard factual fun and trivia-mad nuggets of gold I could alchemically conjure along the way and squeeze into this timeline, things that I hadn't included in *Agents of Fortune*. As well, as the chronology built to epic Godzilla proportions, I found myself appreciating the timeline as a bit of a reference work, which shouldn't have been surprising, because that has always been the case with these books I call "timeline and quotes."

Still, I mean, even though there's lots here to entertain and educate, I definitely urge you to obtain and devour every last page of *Agents of Fortune* — I guarantee you that you will learn lots and come away beguiled, redeemed. But again, by the same token, I'm pretty darn sure that this book will get repeated use even over and above that one, even though on the face of it it's masquerading as a sumptuous coffee table book to display what these guys got up to live, and then of course with the products and the promotional items thereof.

And therein lies my real joy with doing this book.

I mean, long story — let's not get into it — but I've actually started

doing illustrations of Blue Öyster Cult record advertisements, for Cronos' sake, some of them faithful renditions of the ads that might've occurred in those British music weeklies, some complete flights of fancy. That's how nuts I am about Blue Öyster Cult visuals. This dubious use of my time aside, my real joy in terms of being involved with this book is seeing the seven-inch picture sleeves, the promotional items and more than anything, all those great advertisements — the pictures, the ad copy, sometimes rudimentary and charmed, sometimes elaborate and well beyond the embodiment of the record touted. Sure, we all appreciate these things in full colour, but I'm even right chuffed to see the old newsprint ads reproduced in four-colour process, where they pop just a little more magical than the way I've always done them in my lesser and messier trade paperback books.

I may be biased, but I really do believe that a picture book of all things Blue Öyster Cult beats a picture book of almost any other band and their booty. And again, because I really don't like picture books without words, I think Wymer and myself have come up with a concept that adds meat to the bones, more than sufficient and substantial literary content to the beastly feast for the eyes that is the powerful BÖC.

One point of process I'd like to explain — and this is the way I've done it in all my timeline books — any entries that are no more specific than a year go at the beginning of that year. If it's just year and month, it goes at the beginning of that month. Anything dated down to the day (the lion's share of entries), those go chronologically where you would expect them.

To add a few personal reflections... what is my favourite Blue Öyster Cult album, I hear you asking? (!). Well, that would be *Mirrors*, a truly contrarian choice, which is why you can go to YouTube right now and see me argue as such on our YouTube show The Contrarians. Seriously, I know it's a strange choice, but my point, which you will glean from that episode, is that *Mirrors* was the first time the band truly delivered a powerful high fidelity sound, even if it's not the heaviest album in the band's catalogue. Plus the *Mirrors* tour was the first time I saw the band, an event that I gratuitously popped into our timeline. But yes, that happened on vacation way across the country, with my brother Brad (sadly, now deceased), and mom and dad (still with us).

Second time felt much more rock 'n' roll, when me and a few buddies piled into my purple 1977 Toyota Celica and drove south from Trail, BC to Spokane, Washington to catch the band on the *Fire of Unknown Origin* tour, July 11th, 1981, supported by Pat Travers. First damn time I ever met a rock star, too, when I got Eric Bloom to sign a dollar bill for me in the elevator at the hotel on the way to the hallowed hockey barn of that nondescript town of unremarkable size.

Anyway, enough reminiscing — let's get on with the show. I know you're going to love what you see, and I'm pretty sure you're going to appreciate what there is to read here as well.

Martin Popoff
martinp@inforamp.net; martinpopoff.com

"We got a contract, we did the first Cult album, and we decided on the Cult name about a week later. We had about eight names. We couldn't agree. But that was par for the course. We're not really the same kind of guys at all; we never agree on anything. So a couple of the names we were considering were Big Bullet, The Santos Sisters, The Night Wailing; Scumbags was proposed. We had to sign the contract the next day, so we said to Sandy, 'Okay, pick something.' 'The Blue Öyster Cult.' The what? It turned out to be the name of one of Sandy's songs, which eventually became 'Subhuman.'"
Donald "Buck Dharma" Roeser

Origins Through the 1970s

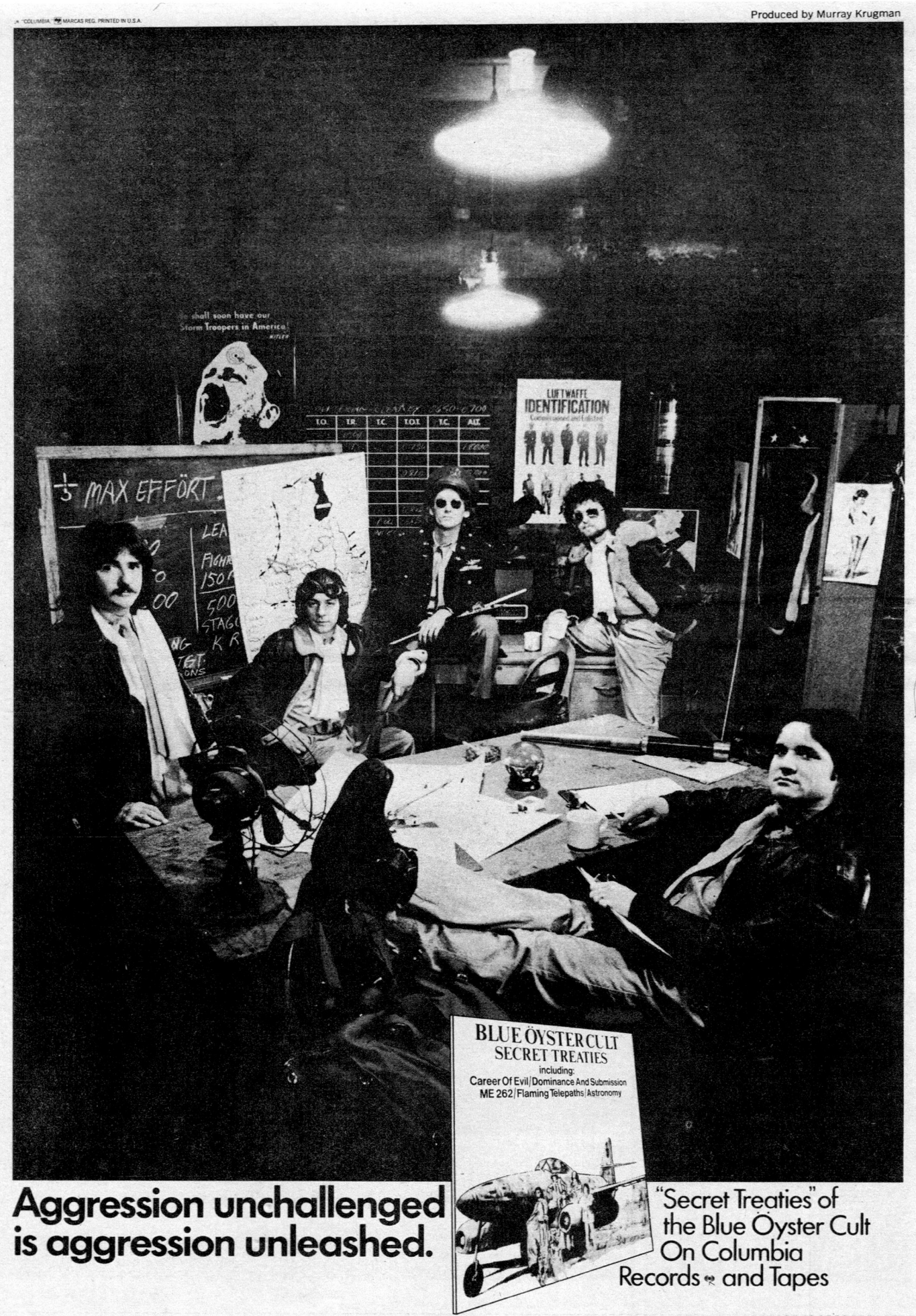

Your intrepid author is back again so soon — did you miss me? — to say a few words about the first section of our book, concentrating on the band's pre-history and what they got up to in the seventies. As it turns out, and as any self-respecting Blue Öyster Cult fan knows, half the damn career is the seventies, and there's nothing wrong with that.

But it's pretty amusing how this band started out. Essentially, it looks like if they had their way, they would've been a psychedelic rock band woefully too late to make anything of themselves. To be sure, they were a bit weird, but not weird enough. They got really weird and incredibly interesting when Sandy Pearlman got involved, and then darker and heavier when it was decided by Columbia that they needed their own Black Sabbath and these Grateful Dead flashbacks just might be the ticket.

Soon the band was toiling away working on the fanciful tracks that would comprise their exotic black-and-white album trilogy, namely *Blue Öyster Cult*, *Tyranny and Mutation* and *Secret Treaties*. Aided and abetted by a New York rock press that could get behind anything heavy from close to home, as well as the band's cerebral lyrics, Buck and Eric grew in stature steadily, punctuating their early seventies rise with a fine yet grimly workmanlike double live album in '75 called *On Your Feet or On Your Knees*.

The band's audience was built on the same principle that made successful the likes of Rush, Styx, Uriah Heep, Foghat, Wishbone Ash, Kiss, Heart, Pat Travers, Aerosmith, Sammy Hagar, Kansas, Ted Nugent and even Black Oak Arkansas, unlikely as that should have been. The idea was to hammer hard everybody in the Midwest and wait for the coasts to catch up. Blue Öyster Cult had the advantage of being from New York and, again, charming the city folk with lyrical missives from the likes of Patti Smith, Richard Meltzer, Helen Wheels, Jim Carroll and Sandy Pearlman. Those other guys started a few steps behind, but to the chagrin of Buck and Eric, a few of them would soon bound past BÖC forthrightly, demonstrating to the Long Island crew that they should be a little more "Buck's Boogie" and a little less "She's as Beautiful as a Foot."

But then as the cards would have it (see album cover), BÖC found themselves fumbling toward ecstasy with 1976's *Agents of Fortune*, which contained not much of anything that mattered to middle America other than smash hit "(Don't Fear) The Reaper." Now they were hockey barn headliners in their own right, and 1977's *Spectres* maintained the momentum, going gold, giving us "R. U. Ready 2 Rock" and "Godzilla," while — surprise — the ballads failed.

Single LP live album *Some Enchanted Evening* was a leftfield success, but then again, live albums were in their golden element at this time. And you didn't necessarily have to put on a two-LP gatefold buffet spread. Foghat scored themselves a nice double platinum hit with 1977's *Live*, and then Judas Priest continued their ascendance with *Unleashed in the East* two years later, as did Pat Travers with *Live! Go for What You Know*.

Still, it makes no sense that *Some Enchanted Evening* is the band's best-selling album, although I'm sceptical that's still the case, given that we've lost the ability to count properly. My theory is that the continued pop culture engagement with "Reaper" as time goes on must surely mean that *Agents of Fortune* is the BÖC record that has "sold" (downloaded, streamed?) the most. I mean, I've always kinda had it in for *Some Enchanted Evening*, because it's somewhat of a mess. The covers, the jamming, not many songs... it ain't no *Unleashed in the East*, I'll tell ya that much.

As the seventies come to a close, the band experience a bit of a dip

with *Mirrors* (maybe they should have called it *Lasers*), which is the first record in a while not to go gold or beyond, although the band maintain their sense of career where it matters, and that's playing to lots and lots of people in hockey arenas. Whether it's A-cities or B-cities is of no matter; this is a working band, establishing the working plan they use to this day. As it happens, they are fully able to maintain a good living as the seventies come to a close, despite the decrease in record sales.

In summary, like I say, all of these fantastic and varied and creatively brave records that Blue Öyster Cult crafted for us… well, they establish the legend of the band, the timelessness of the band and the interest from smart people that records like these should sensibly generate — and for that we thank them. Their career hiccup however also creates the foundation for a sense of crankiness, a particular New Yorker cynicism.

Still, I mean, the guys have to know that it's their own fault, at least a little bit. What they were doing was bound to sail over the heads of the average idiot rock fan. As much as they could (and would) grouse that Kiss and Aerosmith and even Fleetwood Mac were happily bouncing past Blue Öyster Cult with respect to record sales, they must have known that they were just too smart for the masses. I've heard this from the Judas Priest guys as well, and with both bands, I just wish that they would look at the glass as half-full. Gold and platinum with regularity… for God's sake, that's pretty darn good for songs about UFOs, biker gangs and a Lovecraft-steeped story about the occult origins of World War I.

Out Now On Columbia Records And Tapes.

1804 – 1969

August 1804. Imaginos, a "modified child," is born in New Hampshire — or so says Sandy Pearlman, spinner of the tale that would wind its way throughout the canon of the Blue Öyster Cult.

November 1830. Stendhal sees the publication, in two volumes, of his novel *Le Rouge et le Noir: Chronique du XIX siècle*.

August 20, 1890. Howard Phillips Lovecraft is born, in Providence, Rhode Island. His recurring Cthulhu Mythos storyline regarding ancient beings, "old gods that will return," as it were, would reverberate through the lyrical canon of Blue Öyster Cult, first through the musings of Sandy Pearlman, then brought back by John Shirley.

1895. F. Tennyson Neely issues a collection of Robert W. Chambers short stories called *The King in Yellow*. The story called "The King in Yellow" is actually about a fictional book called *The King in Yellow*. Lovecraft had is own fictional work in the *Necronomicon*, and of course, Sandy Pearlman uses this device as well. Additionally, the anthology contains a story called "The Street of the Four Winds," which bears similarity to a lyric in "Astronomy." "E.T.I. (Extra Terrestrial Intelligence)" includes the line, "king in yellow, queen in red."

September 7, 1907. The Cliff House, pictured on the cover of the *Imaginos* album, is destroyed by fire.

August 22, 1914. The Battle of Rossignol, an early skirmish that was part of World War I occurs on this date. Sandy Pearlman's *Imaginos* saga in part posits occult causes to the origins of World War I. As part of the tale, he conjures a fictitious book by "Rossignol" called *The Origins of a World War*.

January 25, 1921. This date marks the premiere of Karel Capek's science fiction play *Rossumovi Univezaini Roboti*, or *Rossum's Universal Robots*. Also known as *R.U.R.*, it is credited as the work that introduced the word robot to the English language. The title of the Blue Öyster Cult song "R. U. Ready 2 Rock" is a tribute to the play, from Sandy Pearlman, sole lyricist on the track, Sandy being a huge fan of early scientific discovery.

March 4, 1922. Silent expressionist horror film *Nosferatu: A Symphony of Horror* begins appearing in movie houses. Blue Öyster Cult would conjure a well-regarded song called "Nosferatu" for inclusion on the 1977 album *Spectres*. The citing of what was written in the captain's log represents a direct reference to the movie.

August 5, 1943. Samuel Clarke Pearlman, a.k.a. Memphis Sam, Sandy Pearlman, is born, Rockaway, Queens, NY. Sandy says he grew up in Lovecraft country, Western Massachusetts, indicating that his family had 200 acres on the Connecticut River, which Lovecraft called the Miskatonic River. His Lovecraft scholarship would prove significant in his lyrics that pertain to the Imaginos Mythos, which is spread across many Blue Öyster Cult albums.

December 1, 1944. Eric Bloom is born, in Brooklyn, NY.

May 10, 1945. Author, pioneering rock critic and BÖC lyricist Richard Meltzer in born, in New York City.

June 25, 1946. Allen Lanier, the hip downtown guy in the band, is born, in Long Island, NY.

December 30, 1946. Patti Smith is born, in Chicago, IL. Patti would become Allen Lanier's girlfriend, and pen a number of BÖC lyrics.

May 24, 1947. Albert Bouchard is born, in Watertown, NY. This is also Bob Dylan's birthday, and as such, Patti Smith includes the date in her lyric for "The Revenge of Vera Gemini." On his 25th birthday, Patti gave Albert the lyric to add to one of his musical compositions proposed for the album.

June 14, 1974. As legend has it, a UFO crashes at a US Air Force base in Roswell, New Mexico (officials identify the craft as nothing more than a weather balloon). What becomes known as the Roswell Incident serves as inspiration for a Blue Öyster Cult song called "Lips in the Hills."

November 12, 1947. Donald "Buck Dharma" Roeser is born, in Long Island, NY.

November 9, 1948. Joe Bouchard is born, like his brother, in Watertown, NY.

May 6, 1949. Helen "Helen Wheels" Robbins is born, in Queens, NY. Albert's girlfriend in college, she would go on to pen the lyrics to "Tattoo Vampire."

November 3, 1954. Godzilla is unleashed upon Tokyo, through the movie of the same name.

July 1956. Jazz legend Charles Mingus issues an album called *Pithecanthopus Erectus*, the title of which has some bearing on BÖC calling their seventh album *Cultosaurus Erectus*.

September 5, 1957. Jack Kerouac sees publication of *On the Road*, a key influence on the song "Burnin' for You." As well, one of his famed works is *The Dharma Bums* — Sandy's conjured alias for Donald is Buck Dharma.

1963. Eric Bloom discovers the music of upstate NY R&B outfit Wilmer and the Dukes, and goes on to see them live over a hundred times. The die is cast.

July 1, 1963. Death of French writer Louis-Ferdinand Celine, inspiration for the song "Searchin' for Celine." His most famous work was novel *Journey to the End of the Night*, a BÖC title if there ever was one.

September 18, 1963. The Roger Corman-directed *X: The Man with the X-Ray Eyes*, starring Ray Milland, hits theatres. The film serves as the inspiration for John Shirley's "X-Ray Eyes" lyric.

December 31, 1963 – January 1, 1964. The abduction story told in "Dominance and Submission" takes place.

March 21, 1964. Future BÖC bassist Danny Miranda is born, in New York.

1965. Eric Bloom, in college, forms some of his first bands. His most notable early act is called Lost and Found.

1966. Sandy Pearlman receives a BA from the State University of New York at Stony Brook. He conceives of a band to perform his lyrics. The name "Soft White Underbelly" is taken from a Winston Churchill World War II speech. However, *Imaginos* will be about the occult origins of the First World War.

1967. Albert Bouchard and Helen Wheels become an item, meeting at a Ravi Shankar concert. She would soon be designing the band's stage clothes.

1967. Sandy Pearlman becomes one of the original rock music journalists, when he begins writing for Paul Williams' Crawdaddy, along with another BÖC lyricist/conceptualist, Richard Meltzer. Blue Öyster Cult would become that rare species: a "heavy metal" band accepted by the critics.

Early 1967. Blue Öyster Cult forms, on Long Island, NY, going under a number of goofy pre-BÖC monikers. The original lineup consists of Donald Roeser on guitar and lead vocals, John Wiesenthal on guitar, Andrew Winters on bass, Allen Lanier on keyboards and Albert Bouchard on drums. For a period, Jeff Latham is in on keyboards but into 1968, the band solidifies around Allen.

Spring 1967. Eric Bloom graduates college, with a BA in modern languages.

Summer 1967. Eric's band Rock Garden gigs around upstate New York, but by the end of July, is broken up. Eric moves to Provincetown, where he panhandles and gets a job washing dishes.

September 1, 1967. Eric gets the call from his friend John Trivers to come play a gig in Clayton, NY the next night and Bloom leaves Provincetown. Lost and Found reforms.

December 1967. Les Braunstein joins the band, on lead vocals and rhythm guitar, making the band a five-piece.

August 28, 1968. The band perform a showcase gig at the Hotel Diplomat Ballroom in New York City for Jac Holzman from Elektra.

Late 1968. Eric "Manny" Bloom, working at Sam Ash, makes the acquaintance of Donald, Allen and Andrew Winters.

Late 1968. Blue Öyster Cult (as Soft White Underbelly), record an album's worth of wobbly psych rock material for Elektra Records, who think they have the second coming of The Grateful Dead on their hands. The album is shelved when the band loses their lead singer a few months later.

November 29, 1968. Eric is asked to provide and run the PA for the band's gig at The Electric Circus in New York.

December 1968. Eric moves into the BÖC band house in Great Neck, NY, first serving as tour manager.

May 1969. Lead singer Les Braunstein quits and is replaced by Eric Bloom.

July 3, 1969. Eric plays his first gig with the band, at the Fillmore East in New York, after a warm-up show at a debutante's 16th birthday party in Riverside, Connecticut back in May.

July – September 1969. The band work at CBS Studios in Manhattan on tracks that wouldn't emerge until the 2001 reissue of *Blue Öyster Cult*.

August 1969. Elektra issues a Tom Paxton album called *The Things I Notice Now*. Albert Bouchard drums on one track.

December 6, 1969. The infamous Altamont concert headlined by the Rolling Stones in California, at which a concert-goer named Meredith Hunter got stabbed to death. The Hells Angels had been hired as security. BÖC wrote a song about the festival-gone-wrong called "Transmaniacon M.C," which would show up on the band's debut album.

1970

1970. *The Aesthetics of Rock* by Richard Meltzer sees publication. It is considered the first serious book of rock criticism. Meltzer would pen the lyrics for fully nine Blue Öyster Cult songs spanning four decades, as well as songs for The Brain Surgeons.

February – May 1970. The band, at this point The Stalk-Forrest Group (and previously, briefly Oaxaca), work at Elektra Sound Recorders in New York and Los Angeles on a second set of songs for another proposed album. They would finally be dropped by Elektra and resurface with a new name on Columbia.

February 13, 1970. Black Sabbath issue their debut album, which includes "The Wizard," soon to be turned inside out by BÖC and emerge as "Cities on Flame with Rock and Roll."

Summer 1970. Albert Bouchard's little brother Joe joins the band, replacing Andrew Winters. The guys at first didn't think Joe was cool enough but he soon becomes both a writer and occasional lead singer to augment his bass guitar role.

September 3, 1970. Joe does his first gig with the band, playing on the back of a flatbed truck in Great Neck on Long Island. The band is still known as Stalk-Forrest Group. Then it's on to the infamous Swingers' Naturalist Party up at Camp Swan Lake, Swan Lake, NY.

December 31, 1970. The band's New Years Eve gig is at Conry's East in Farmingdale, NY, the name of the place to be immortalized in "Before the Kiss, a Redcap."

1971

September 1971. The band formerly known as Soft White Underbelly, Oaxaca, Stalk-Forrest Group and just Stalk-Forrest becomes the much riffier Blue Öyster Cult, which gets signed to Columbia, after auditioning this year. But it's gradual, including concert billings as "BÖC" and even a reversion back to Stalk-Forrest.

October 1971. Blue Öyster Cult, working at The Warehouse in New York, record the tracks that will comprise their debut album. It is said that Columbia wanted their own version of Black Sabbath, currently burning up the charts over at Warner Bros. Between the label brass, manager Sandy Pearlman and a band eager to make it, BÖC get both spookier and heavier than they were in their hippie days.

1972

January 17, 1972. Blue Öyster Cult issue their debut album, a self-titled, on Columbia. The cover art is by the mysterious Bill Gawlik, an architecture student at SUNY who soon disappears for good.

Spring 1972. Albert begins writing music for Sandy's Imaginos Mythos, the project eventually seeing the light of day sixteen years later.

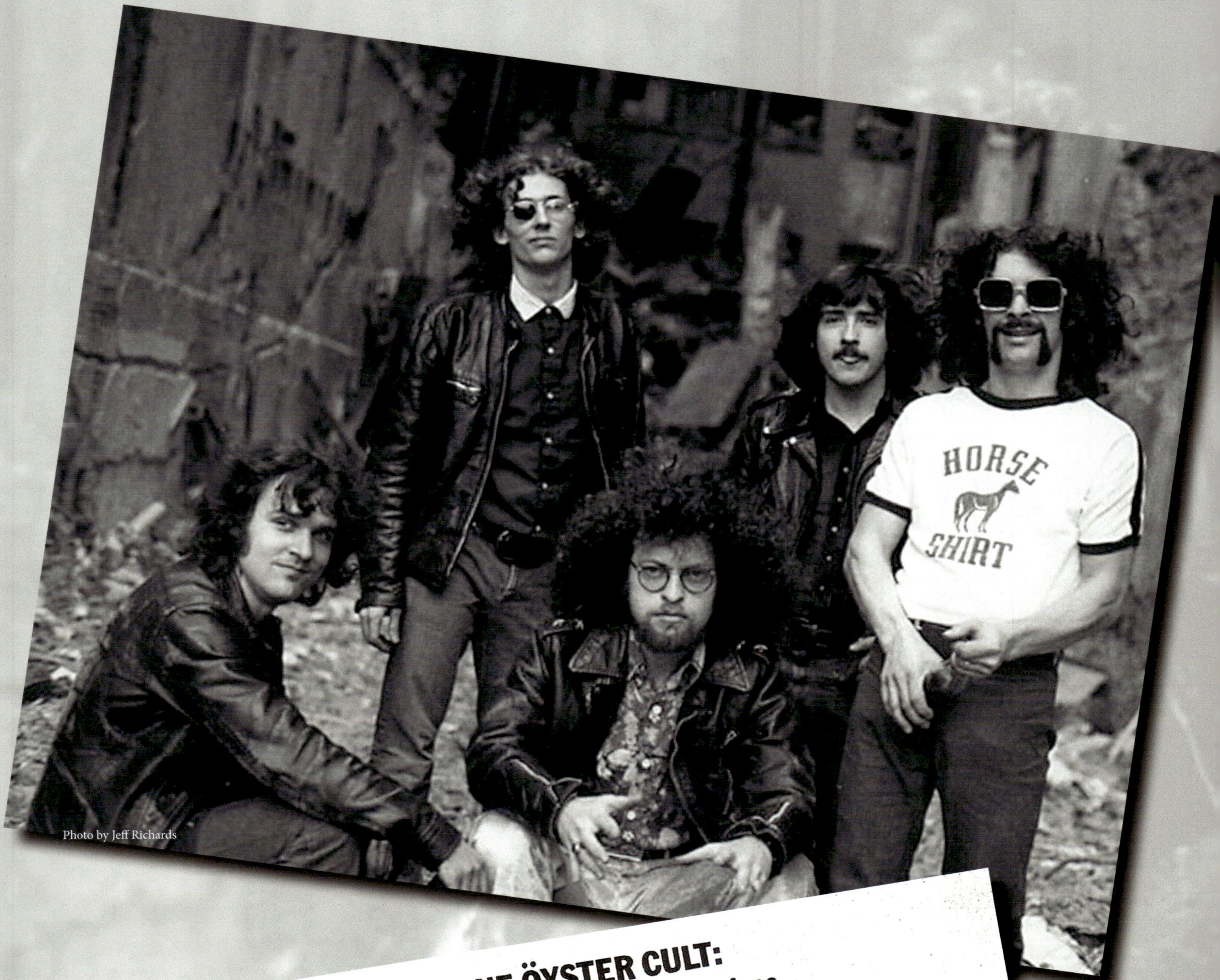

Photo by Jeff Richards

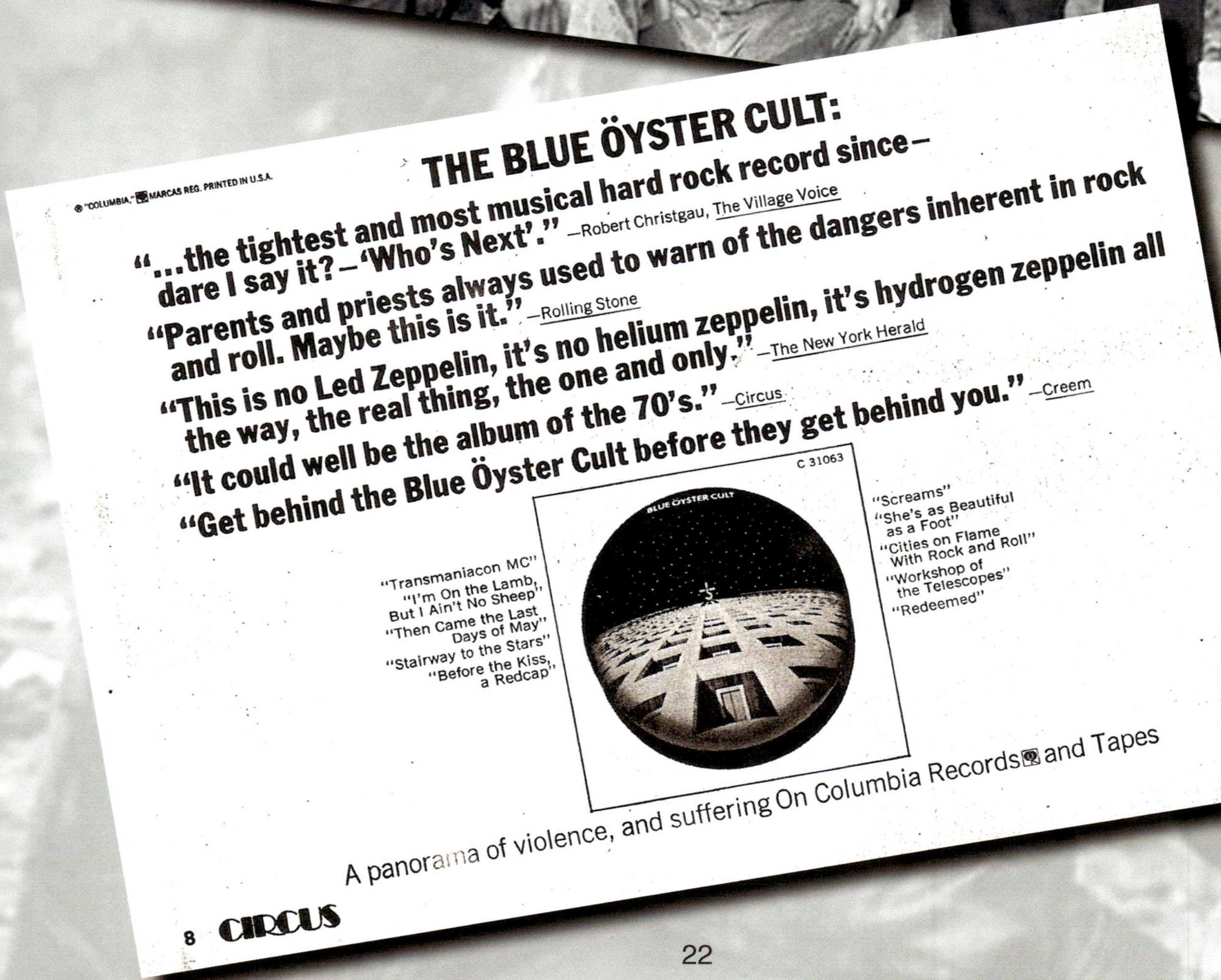

THE BLUE ÖYSTER CULT:

"...the tightest and most musical hard rock record since— dare I say it?—'Who's Next'." —Robert Christgau, The Village Voice

"Parents and priests always used to warn of the dangers inherent in rock and roll. Maybe this is it." —Rolling Stone

"This is no Led Zeppelin, it's no helium zeppelin, it's hydrogen zeppelin all the way, the real thing, the one and only." —The New York Herald

"It could well be the album of the 70's." —Circus

"Get behind the Blue Öyster Cult before they get behind you." —Creem

"Transmaniacon MC"
"I'm On the Lamb, But I Ain't No Sheep"
"Then Came the Last Days of May"
"Stairway to the Stars"
"Before the Kiss, a Redcap"

"Screams"
"She's as Beautiful as a Foot"
"Cities on Flame With Rock and Roll"
"Workshop of the Telescopes"
"Redeemed"

A panorama of violence, and suffering On Columbia Records and Tapes

March 3, 1972. The band audition for the opportunity to join Alice Cooper's concert dates conducted just before *School's Out* comes out. They pass muster and tour up and down the Eastern Seaboard with Alice in April and May.

April 5, 1972. Blue Öyster Cult booking agent Phil King (real name: Phil Friedman) is chased out of a diner into the street (and eventually to the front door of a house) and shot in the head three times and dies, in a dispute over gambling debts owed to him. Phil is remembered fondly for his big moustache, sunglasses, fashion flair and '64 Lincoln Continental, as well as his success in getting local radio to play "Cities on Flame with Rock and Roll" as soon as the first record came out.

April 21, 1972. "Cities on Flame with Rock and Roll," backed with "Before the Kiss, a Recap," is issued as a single, picture sleeve for the promo, non-PS for the commercial issue.

May 20, 1972. Spurred by the new single and good notices in the burgeoning rock press, the self-titled debut makes the charts, reaching #172.

June – December 1972. After the Alice Cooper dates, the band tour hard for the balance of the year, essentially in the eastern half of the country, jumping on for isolated dates with a large variety of bands while playing multiple dates with Big Brother and the Holding Company in June and Black Sabbath in July.

> **BLUE OYSTER CULT: (CBS 64904)**
> THIS IS the much-vaunted American band composed, I believe, of rock and roll critics — and certainly championed by them as *the* underground band. Its cult appeal has been carefully fostered, and if this is what happens when the men who write the reviews get behind the instruments, then I can only say: Back to your typewriters! It's a dense, hard, riffy music without great finesse... but then finesse is not what punk-rock is about, I suppose. Lead, guit arist Donald Roeser wails away over some powerful, churning rhythms from a thick, unsubtle rhythm section. There appear to be three guitarists and it all gets a bit overbearing at times, though really there are some nice touches — "Then Came The Last Days Of May" is based on a pleasing idea and when they tone it down, give each other some room, exploit the use of space a little, then the music becomes quite acceptable. "Redeemed" is nice, with more intelligent use of dynamics, but most of the rest is undistinguished, like trying to tell the difference between being hit on the head with a ten-pound hammer and a twenty-pound hammer — either way it gets to you. This album was recorded way back in October 1971, though it has only just been released by CBS, so I would imagine most of the people who wanted it would have it by now. I don't want to give the impression that this is a rotten album — the playing never drops below competent, but it's the competence of slightly outdated heavy-psychedelic rock or whatever, as indicated by the hippy-trippy name. Maybe it's meant to be a bit of a joke, and as for the bit about the critics ... actually they are probably all musicians doing the best they can, but there's a score of British bands who have got albums out who can better this. Put it down to a White Elephant Craze. — M.H.

1973

1973. Future BÖC drummer Rick Downey is hired as Albert's drum tech.

February 11, 1973. Columbia issues the second Blue Öyster Cult album, *Tyranny and Mutation*. "Hot Rails to Hell"/"7 Screaming Dizbusters" is issued as a picture sleeve single. "The Red and the Black"/"Baby Ice Dog" is issued as a single as well, but only in Japan. The cover art, which Sandy compares to Third Reich architect Albert Speer's city of the future concept, is the second and last for the band by Bill Gawlik, commonly known as Gawlik.

June 15, 1973. Invaluable soundman George Geranios joins the team at a gig in Jacksonville, Florida. He stays exclusive with BÖC through 1984.

October 14, 1973. The band play their first show in Canada, at the venerable Massey Hall in Toronto, supporting Mott the Hoople and Aerosmith.

December 31, 1973. Kiss play the show that is widely considered their first, or at least their "industry debut." The gig takes place at the Academy of Music in New York City, and also features Iggy and the Stooges, Teenage Lust and headliner Blue Öyster Cult. Exactly two years later, BÖC would be supporting Kiss, at a Nassau Coliseum show.

Albert, Joe and Iggy Pop.

1974

1974. Columbia issue *Tyranny and Mutation* and *Secret Treaties* on eight-track tape and as four-channel quadraphonic LPs.

April 5, 1974. *Secret Treaties*, the band's third album, is released. Like *Imaginos*, the packaging includes a cryptic summary statement. As alluded to earlier, it refers to a fictitious book, *The Origins of a World War*, which is essentially what Sandy says *Imaginos* is about, 14 years later. What Imaginos, named Desdinova, does with his life, is succinctly summed up as a "career of evil." His official role in the unspecified war is "the foreign minister." UK's NME rates *Secret Treaties* as the 13th best album of the year. "Career of Evil"/"Dominance and Submission" is issued as a single. "Flaming Telepaths"/"Career of Evil" sees release as a picture sleeve single in Japan. The unsettling cover art, with the dogs (both alive and dead) and Eric in a cape, is reminiscent of Process Church imagery. The working title for *Secret Treaties* was *Power in the Hands of Fools*.

April 27, 1974. The band play a show at the Capitol Theatre in Passaic, New Jersey, with Kiss. BÖC's set is to be immortalized on a live album the following year. Further shows out west are captured in October.

December 31, 1974. At an Academy of Music show in New York, during the encore, Eric fulfills a New Years resolution and shaves off his beard.

Photo: Joe Bouchard Collection

1975

February 27, 1975. BÖC enjoy the release of their first live album, a double with gatefold, called *On Your Feet or On Your Knees*. The album reaches #22 on the Billboard charts. Japan issues a picture sleeve single pairing "Then Came the Last Days of May" with "Cities on Flame with Rock and Roll." The US goes with Steppenwolf cover "Born to Be Wild," which is pressed on both sides, with Japan also taking up "Born to Be Wild" but backing it with "Cities on Flame with Rock and Roll."

March 1975. The celebrated BÖC production team of Sandy Pearlman and Murray Krugman work with "the baby BÖC," namely The Dictators, who issue their debut album *Go Girl Crazy!* at this time. Allen guests on two tracks, "Teengenerate" and "Cars and Girls."

April 4, 1975. Pavlov's Dog issue their debut album, *Pampered Menial*, on ABC Records. It is produced by BÖC team Sandy Pearlman and Murray Krugman, as is the band's second and last (before reunion) record, *At the Sound of the Bell*, in 1976.

September 10, 1975. Kiss *Alive!* is issued. Nothing is ever the same for Kiss and nothing is ever the same for instant huge Kiss fan Danny Miranda, who gives up the saxophone and takes up the guitar (and eventually the bass).

November 10, 1975. Patti Smith's debut album *Horses* includes Allen, Patti's boyfriend at the time, as guest keyboard player and guitarist. Lanier also gets songwriting credits on "Kimberly" and "Elegie".

BLUE ÖYSTER CULT
L to R: Allen Lanier, Eric Bloom, Albert Bouchard, Donald "Buck Dharma" Roeser, Joe Bouchard

© Rich Galbraith

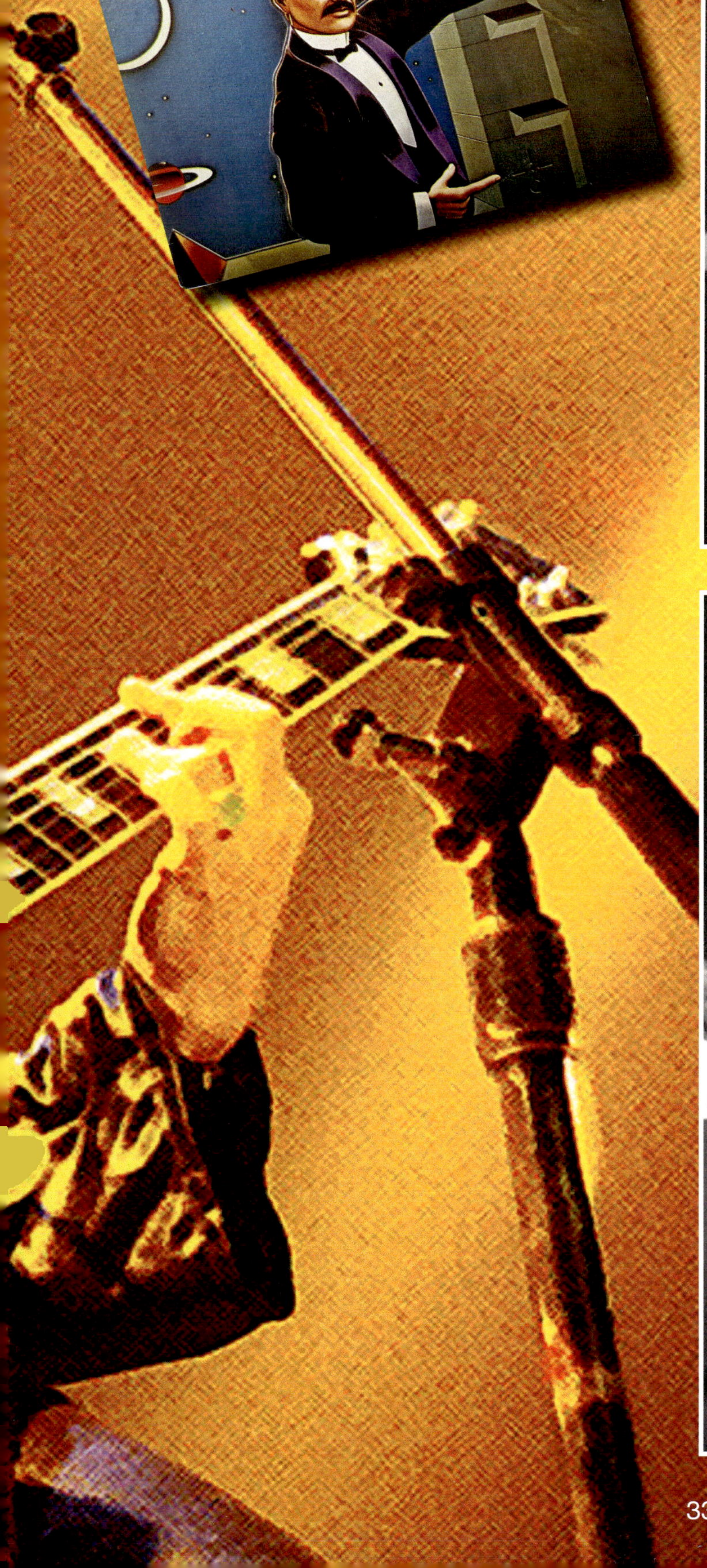

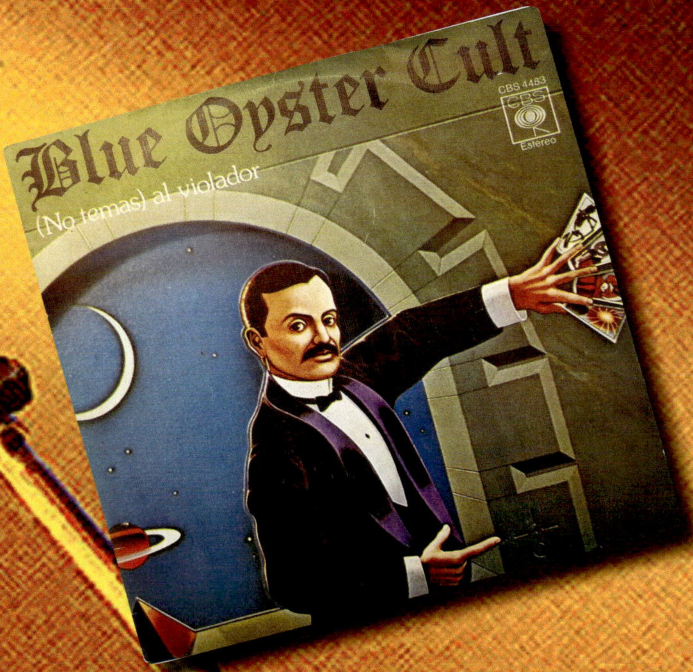
Blue Oyster Cult
(No temas) al violador
CBS 4483
CBS
Estereo

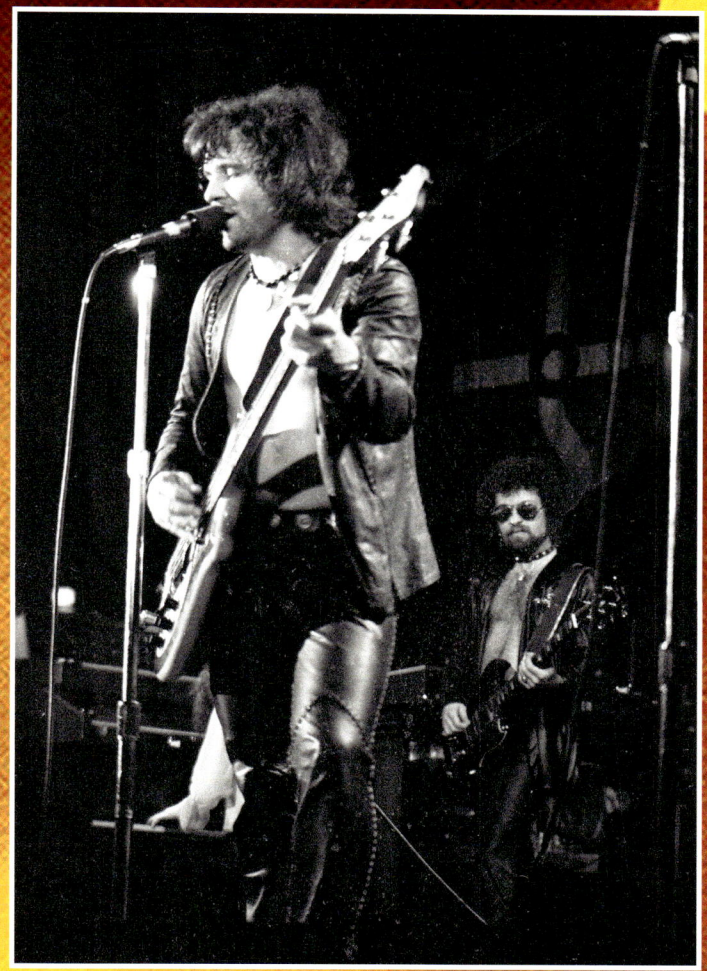

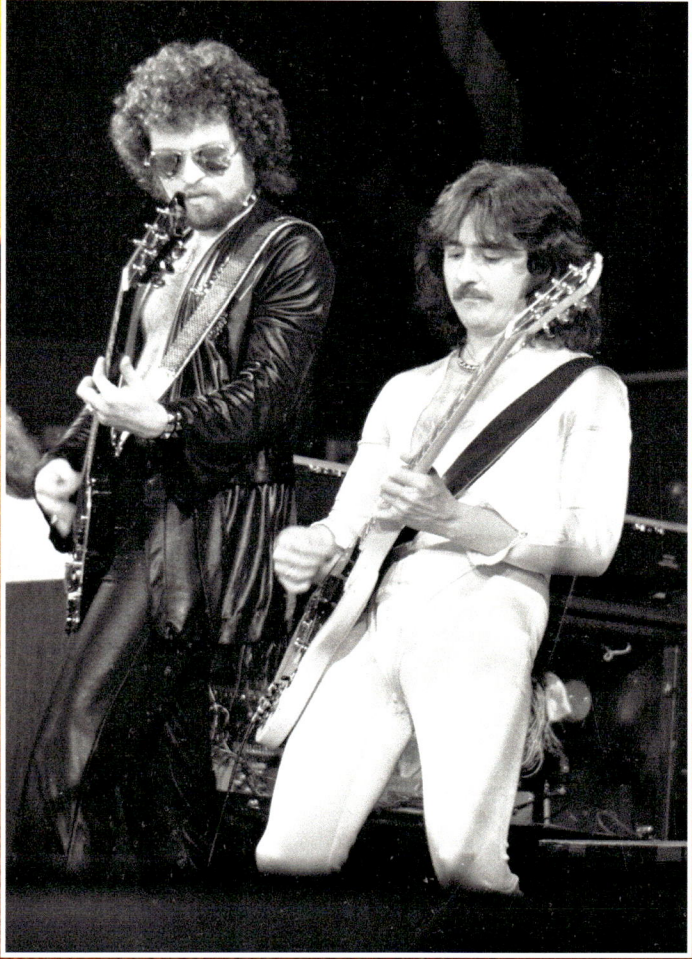

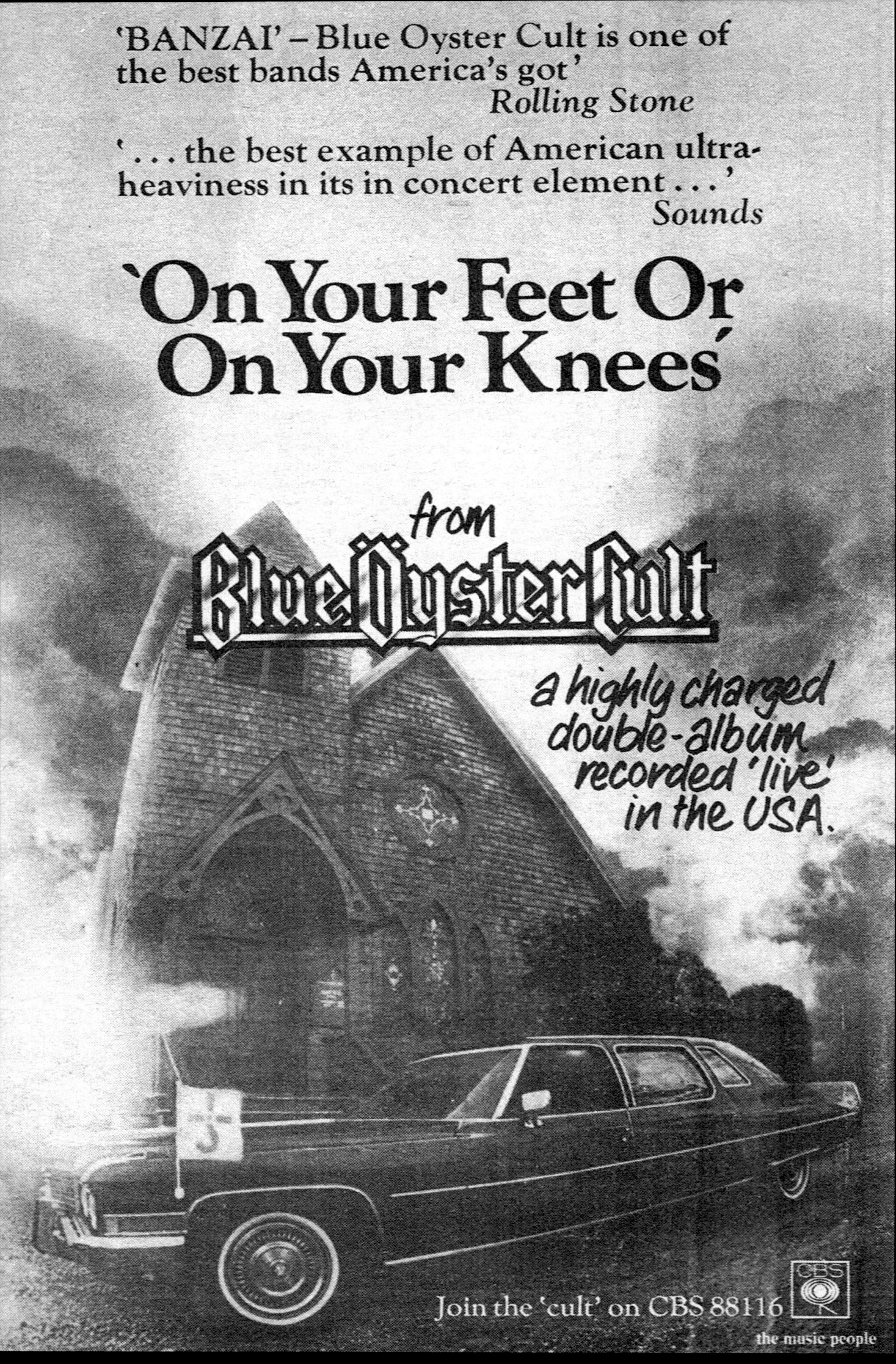

'BANZAI' – Blue Öyster Cult is one of the best bands America's got'
Rolling Stone

'... the best example of American ultra-heaviness in its in concert element...'
Sounds

'On Your Feet Or On Your Knees'

from **Blue Öyster Cult**

a highly charged double-album recorded 'live' in the USA.

Join the 'cult' on CBS 88116

the music people

"This is the fourth great live rock LP ever recorded. The first three being 'Ya Ya's,' 'Live Johnny Winter And,' 'Rock 'n' Roll Animal'(sorry David). It may be the finest ever, 'cause Roxy Music will probably never record one. Not only does this capture the vociferous live aggression of a BÖC concert, but their version of "Born To Be Wild" makes ya want to be 18 again, ridin' down the highway with a tape of this jammed between yer favorite gal's legs."
—*Creem Magazine*

A specially priced 2-record set
Blue Öyster Cult
On Your Feet Or On Your Knees
including:
Cities On Flame/ME 262/Born To Be Wild
Buck's Boogie/I Ain't Got You

On Columbia Records and Tapes.

Produced by Murray Krugman and Sandy Pearlman.

On June 8, the Blue Öyster Cult stars on the King Biscuit Flower Hour.
Check your local listings for time and radio station.

1976

January 1, 1976. A show in Chicago is cancelled as Buck deals with a gallstone.

Spring 1976. The band come off the road at the end of January to work at The Record Plant in New York City on the songs that will comprise their fourth studio album.

May 21, 1976. The band issue the first studio album of their post-black-and-white period. *Agents of Fortune* would go platinum and reach #29 on the Billboard charts on the strength of surprise hit, "(Don't Fear) The Reaper." UK's influential New Musical Express rates the record the sixth best of the year. The cover art painting is by Lynn Curlee, also famous for *Heaven and Hell* by Black Sabbath — in 1980, Sandy would be managing both Black Sabbath and Blue Öyster Cult.

June 1976. "(Don't Fear) The Reaper" is issued as a single, backed with the heaviest song from *Agents of Fortune*, "Tattoo Vampire," lyrics by Helen Wheels who also pens "Sinful Love." "Reaper" vaults to #12 on the Billboard singles chart, also achieving a #16 placement in the UK and #7 in Canada. Japan issues a pictures sleeve single for "Sinful Love," backed with "Reaper". Also floated for radio consumption, "This Ain't the Summer of Love" backed with "Debbie Denise," the latter of which is considered a pop abomination by the Cult faithful.

October 26, 1976. *Agents of Fortune* is certified gold in the US.

December 27, 1976. The band play a gig at the Capitol Centre in Landover, Maryland that gets issued years later on CD as *Live 1976*. This caps a year of intensive touring since May, including tour legs with ZZ Top, Bob Seger and Rush.

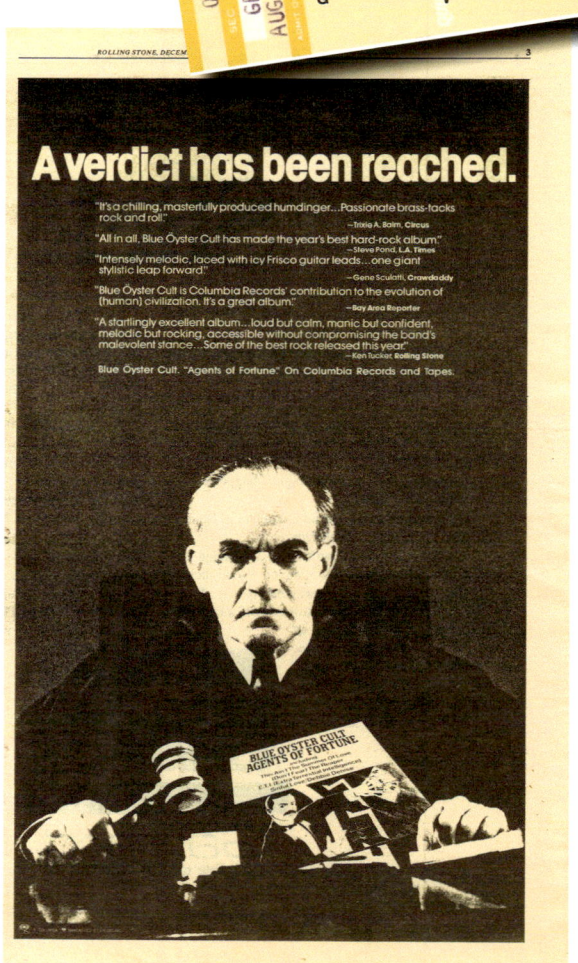

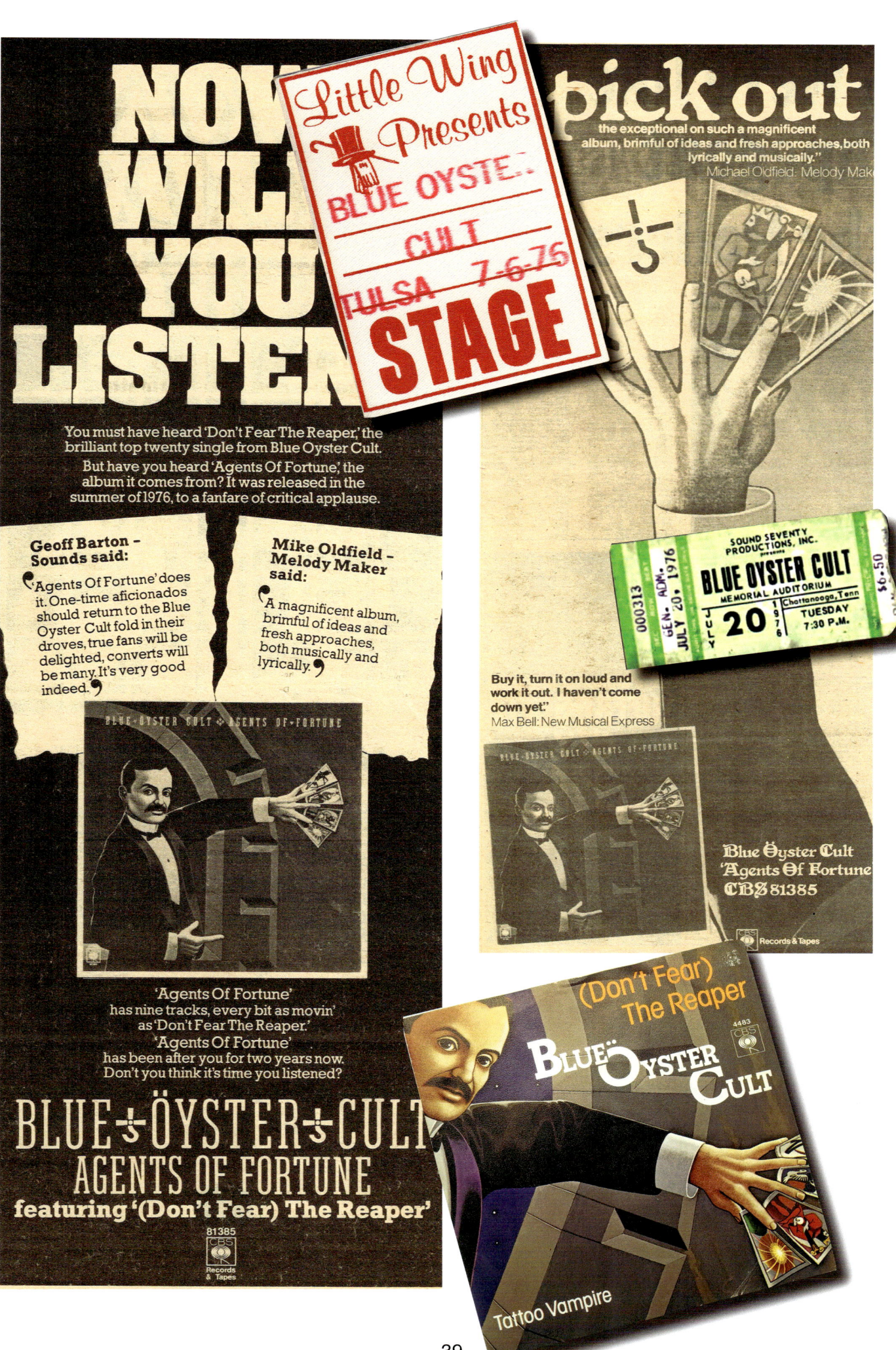

Page 38 SOUNDS November 5, 1977

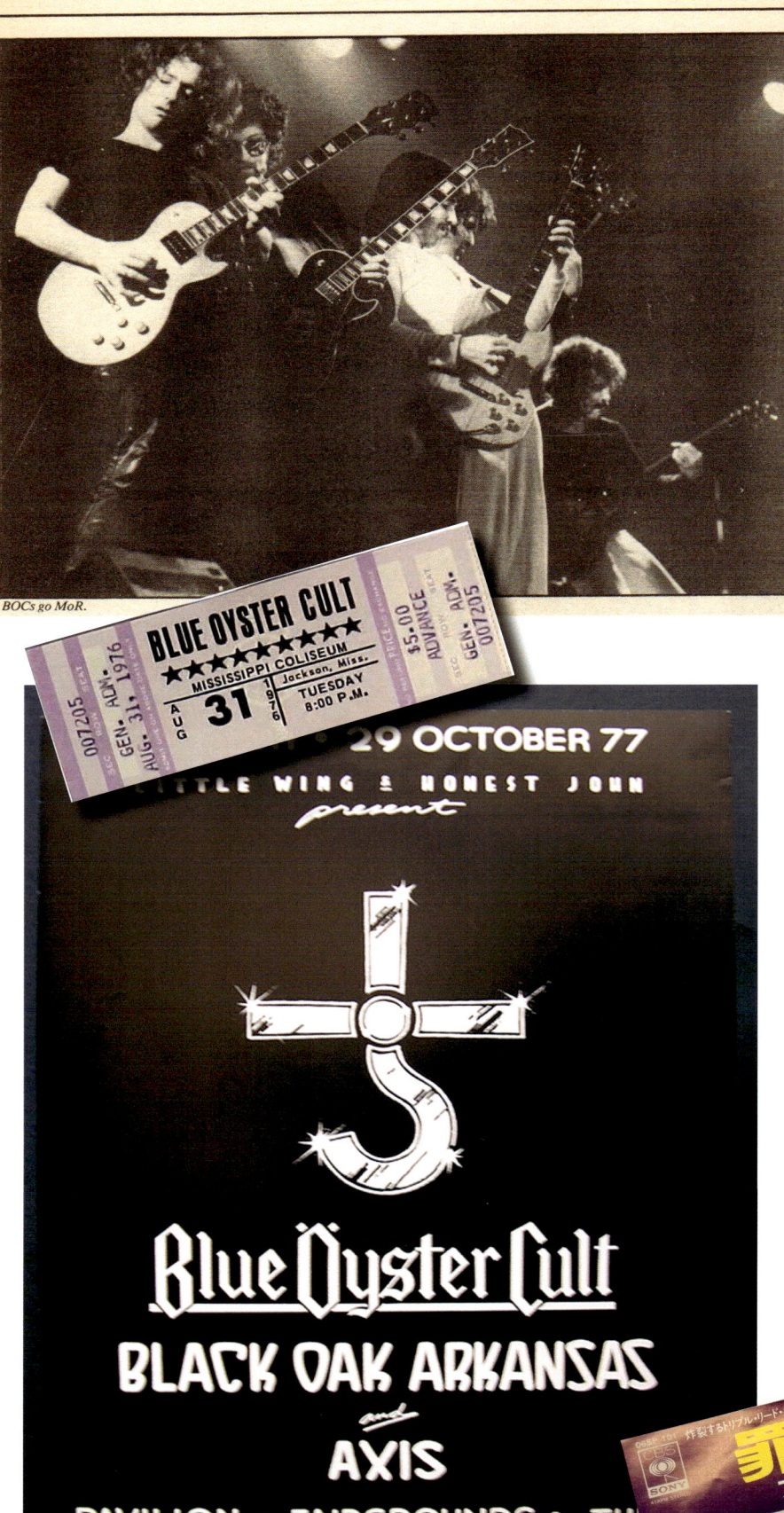

BOCs go MoR.

Cult — ghosts of their former selves

Seafood cocktail ~~up~~

(Note to Melody Maker subs: these headings can be hired o reasonable prices from the address on page 63. They're R Coleman approved!)

BLUE OYSTER CULT
'Spectres'
(Columbia JC 35019 import)**

'... And we're going through the motions,
Yeah we're going through the motions,
Yeah we're going through the motions,
Going through the motions...'
TOO RIGHT.

'Spectres', as far as I'm concerned, is a very disappointing album. Encouraged/obsessed/misguided by the success of the Byrds-like '(Don't Fear) The Reaper' from their last album 'Agents Of Fortune', the Blue Oyster Cult have opted to record what amounts to just about a whole album in the same soft, sensitive, restrained musical fashion. Which is not — repeat not — what I reckon the band's all about, where their musical forté truly lies.

'Agents Of Fortune' was alright for a couple of weeks. Well, more than alright. It was an instantly appealing album, the Cult's most immediately accessible effort ever, and it garnered ecstatic reviews from just about every corner and rightfully so — at the time. Trouble was, 'Agents' became very wearing after a while, it was really too much of a good thing. I don't think I've played it for about a year — for, unlike prevous B. O'Cult albums, I found that it failed to stand the telling test of time. And, probably, a similar fate will befall 'Spectres'.

Whether true, dyed-in-the-wool Cult fans will be able to find some hidden charms in what amounts to a basically low-key album, I don't know. I've always liked the band for their contributions to the heavy rock heritage, have never really been into their decadent lyrical leanings, have never been able to truly comprehend where Cult conviction ends and the tongue-in-cheek pose begins...

However. This particular album has the Cult straying a long, long way away from their original direction/intentins. 'To thee I dedicate this photograph, I'll even sign it, love to you' and

'That night her kiss tol
over, I walked out late
dark, the misty moon s
soak up my sorrows...
these are hardly words
find in a Blue Oyster C
of the past, yet here the
songs — 'Going Throug
Motions' and 'I Love T
gentle, balladic compo
both of them. As are al
'Searching For Celine'
shockingly, surprisingl
me of present-day Gold
Earring', 'Fireworks' a
'Celestial The Queen'.

In 'Spectres', Blue O
rarely come alive with
forcefulness. Donald R
immaculately well thro
[indeed is one of the al
saving graces] but neve
loose in proud 'Buck's
tradition, coming close
'Godzilla', a tribute to
Japanese monster ['Oh
goes Tokyo'], though s
not in 'R.U. Ready 2 r
sadly wimpold workou

Only in 'The Gold
Leather' do the Cult ap
anywhere near their pr
greatness — starting of
short a capella in joke,
develops into a lengthy
somewhat menacing tu
for the reference to 'Th
The Black'] and succe
manages to escape fro
album's overall glossy,
feel.

But, as I say, 'Spectr
a major disappointmen
comparison to much o
earlier work, the Blue
now sound like a bunch
the-hill softies and if th
something about their
sharpish their next LP
stray into Eagles sun,
pools and tequila terri
is, they're dangerously
already.

Personally, I wanna
like 'Dominance And
Submission' [alright!],
[yeah!], 'Hot Rails To
hmm!] or 'Seven Scre
Dizbusters' [yeow!] ag

Unfortunately, at th
all we have to contend
words like 'Desolate la
storybook bliss, my da
tell you this — it's crazy
words a total, tragic b
Now if only someone
explain to me for why.
GEOFF BARTON.
mismanaged 'I Can't

1977

1977. Cape publishes the Adrian Berry book, *Iron Sun: Crossing the Universe Through Black Holes*, which serves as inspiration for BÖC song "Heavy Metal: The Black and Silver."

1977. Krugman and Pearlman team up again for a second Dictators album, called *Manifest Destiny*. Sandy is also the manager of the band. Future BÖC manager Steve Schenck is credited as Production Coordinator.

June 1, 1977. *Agents of Fortune* is certified gold in Canada.

June 16 – 29, 1977. The band conduct their first cross-Canada tour.

July – September 1977. The band work — on and off, frustratingly sporadically — at The Record Plant in Manhattan on tracks for their forthcoming fifth studio album. Having seriously thought about assembling the *Imaginos* concept album since 1975, the band actually write all the songs for the record, only to shelve them for later — much later.

July 15, 1977. *On Your Feet or On Your Knees* is certified gold in the US. It joins the ranks of a number of double live albums from the time considered classics, including Kiss – *Alive!*, *Frampton Comes Alive!*, *All the World's a Stage* from Rush and *Live and Dangerous* from Thin Lizzy.

October – December 1977. BÖC and BOA (Black Oak Arkansas) get together for the first of BÖC's "Black & Blue" tours — more famed as well as infamous is the pairing of BÖC with Black Sabbath in the early eighties.

November 1, 1977. BÖC issue their fifth studio album, *Spectres*. "Goin' Through the Motions," backed with "Searchin' for Celine," is issued as a single. Neither tracks are particular embraced by the fans, with "Godzilla", R. U. Ready 2 Rock" and "Golden Age of Leather" winning out instead.

Late 1977. "I Love the Night"/"Nosferatu" is issued as a UK single from *Spectres*.

December 31, 1977 – June 1, 1978. The band perform the concerts that will generate the material for their second live album. Fans are drawn by the buzz of the band hauling around a delicate and expensive laser system.

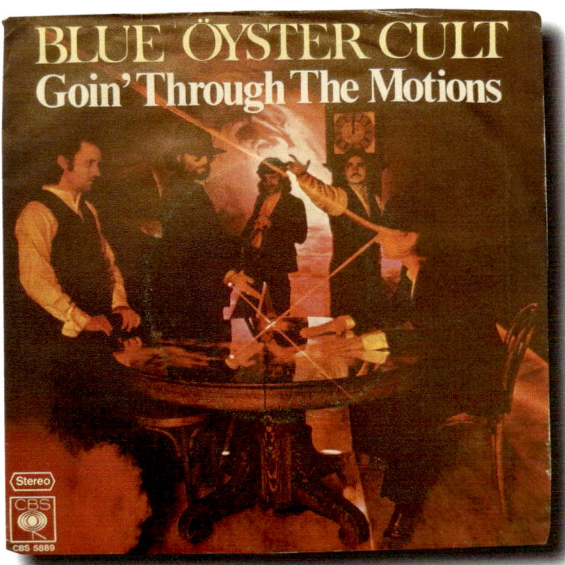

© Rich Galbraith

© Rich Galbraith

47

BACK PAGES

by Peter Crescenti

NEW YORK

BOC: Songwriters Turned Homebodies

The Cult takes on furthering the cause of democratic rock 'n' roll songwriting.

Blue Oyster Cult will begin serious work next month on the follow-up album to their enormously successful 'Agents of Fortune.' Work for the LP will begin with a vacation for the band, when each member will write and record his own songs for the album on home equipment. Then the band will meet for a general rehearsal, and exchange ideas.

"Then we bash it out and see what democracy has to say," Cult vocalist **Eric Bloom** explains. BOC developed their current method of preparing and recording their material while working on 'Agents.' It was the first album the band cut while they were affluent enough to own home recording gear.

"The way we used to write material," Bloom reveals, "is we used to work up just the bare bones of the song and play it for everybody. Then everybody would throw in this and that. That's how we wrote all the other records. But on 'Agents,' it's mostly the way the demos were written is the way the songs appeared on the record."

The Cult drew the tunes for 'Agents' from a source of about two dozen songs, some of which may appear on the next LP. Bloom explained that several leftover tunes were strong, but weren't quite organized enough musically to make the last album. They will be polished up," Eric promises.

One song which has a definite chance of making the new record is **Albert Bouchard's** "Fire of Unknown Origin." It is one of several tunes the drummer wrote based on lyrics or poems penned by BOC soulmate, **Patti Smith**. Bouchard is also writing some conceptual material with BOC's co-producer **Sandy Pearlman**. Currently only in the demo stages, the tunes may come out under the Cult banner.

"That's really a back burner project," says Bloom, "but it's definitely in the offing somewhere down the pike. Everybody is writing all the time. I think we're just starting to hit our stride. After eight years together, we're just starting to see some success."

Since last May, the Cult has played about 23 concerts a month, but from now through March, the group will alternately tour and vacation, in preparation for the next LP. With all the live exposure the group's had, their records are all suddenly turning platinum and gold, prompting the band to shift their careers into high gear.

"There will definitely be changes down the road on every level," Bloom boldly promises. "I don't think you'll be hearing any more of that really hard-edged, heavy metal, sort of 'bad sounding' records from us. We're gonna go for the best producers, the best studios, and make records that sound the best over the radio and on home stereo."

Starz Illuminate Controversial Song

Some material on the new **Starz** album, 'Kneewalkers, Nightcrawlers, and Queers,' due out this month, promises to generate as much controversy as tunes like "Pull The Plug," a song about mercy killing from 'Starz,' the group's debut LP.

"We have censorship problems," claims the group's lead singer **Michael Lee Smith**, "because we like to confront people, and get straight ahead with things, rather than be half-assed. So we run into problems with the lyrics we write.

"There's one on this new album called 'Piss Party,' which is about one of those little 'scenes' in New York. I don't know how people are gonna react to it.

"We played 'Piss Party' one time on the road, in Detroit, and then a couple of nights later we were in Port Huron, Michigan, and people were yelling for it. They heard about it, and they wanted to hear it. But it's kinda been censored already. We've been told we can't sing those lyrics. But we'll work around it. We don't compromise. A lot of our songs are really kind of tongue in cheek, and people don't know if we're smart or stupid or what."

The band finished recording their new LP just last month, co-producing the disk with heavy metal specialist **Jack Douglas**, at New York's Record Plant. Starz'll be touring the States behind the LP through April, and then there's tentative plans for a European tour with **Blue Oyster Cult** in May or June. For a new band, Starz has been incredibly fortunate to introduce themselves to the public via the coliseum route, opening for currently hot acts like BOC. The exposure seems to have turned Starz into an instant success.

"We just want to get out there," says Smith, "and make people aware of us immediately. A lot of bands have to go out and drive around in cars for two years, and play a lot of little gigs.

© Rich Galbraith

51

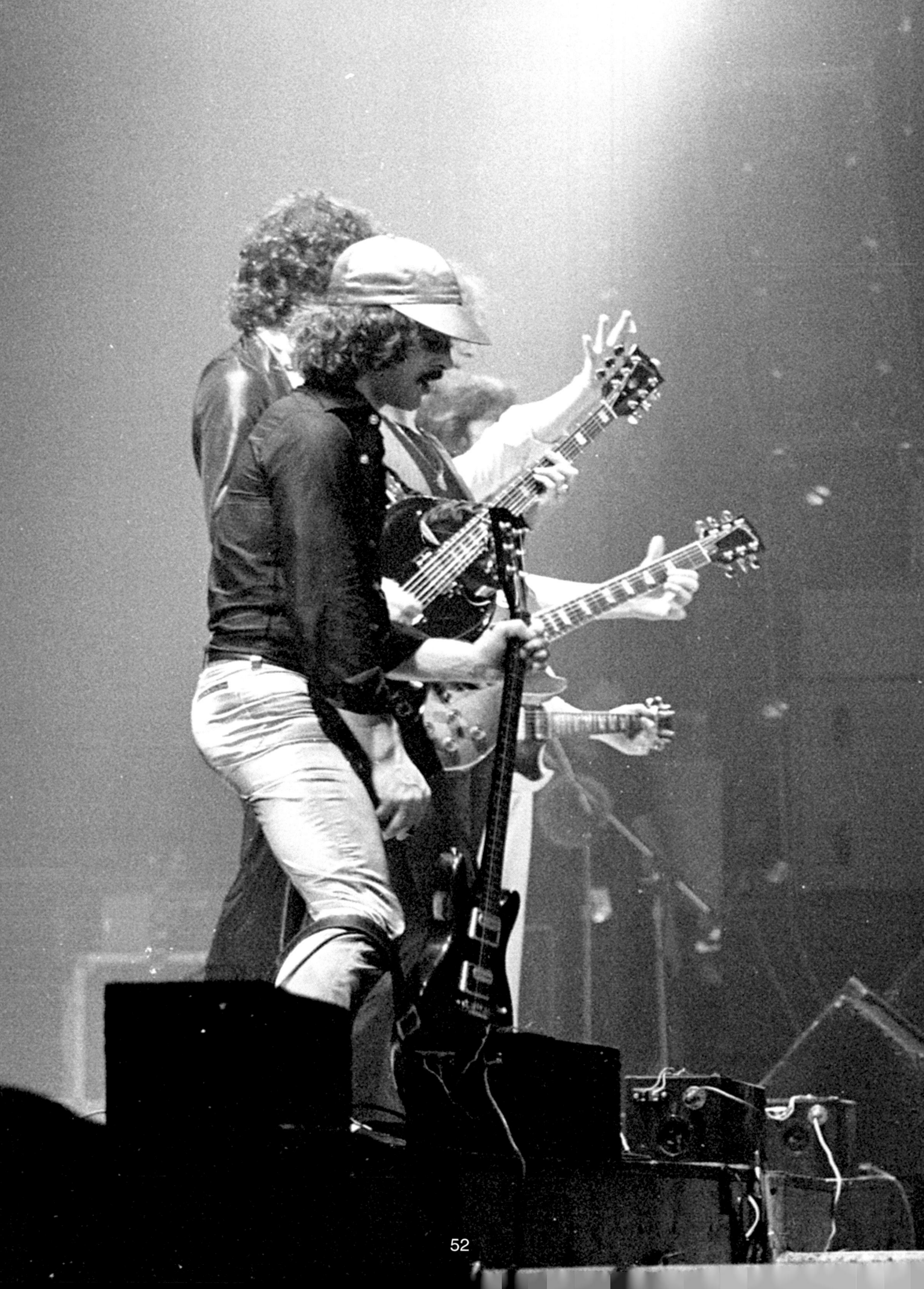

© Rich Galbraith

1978

January 19, 1978. *Spectres* is certified gold, sales driven in part by Albert wearing a Godzilla mask in his drum solo, not to mention the laser show.

February 1978. "Godzilla"/"Nosferatu" is issued as the second single from *Spectres*. Japan switches out "Nosferatu" for "Born to Be Wild."

March 3, 1978. Arista issues a third Patti Smith album. *Easter* includes a cameo by Patti's boyfriend, Allen Lanier, on a song called "Space Monkey."

April 1978. "Godzilla (Live)"/"Godzilla (Studio)" is issued as a single.

April 27, 1978. After the band's usually intensive blanketing of the US early in the year, they play their first ever show in the UK, at Colston Hall in Bristol. The UK leg, supported by post-punk band Japan, is followed by the band's first mainland European dates, supported by Johnny Cougar (later, John Mellencamp). By May 30th, they are back in England, with Japan supporting once again.

May 24, 1978. Cheap Trick issue *Heaven Tonight*, produced by Tom Werman, who will soon be working on Blue Öyster Cult's *Mirrors*. There's a high-pitched babble of voices at 0:55 of the song "How Are You". This is Tom Werman reciting "The Lord's Prayer", which he then sped up. Werman puts the clip into service a second time at 0:33 of "You're Not the One (I Was Looking for)" on the BÖC record.

July 1978. Krugman and Pearlman team up for a third and final (before reunion) Dictators album, called *Bloodbrothers*.

July 17, 1978. *Agents of Fortune* becomes the band's first platinum album, certified this day for sales of over one million copies. The uncharacteristically Byrds-like "(Don't Fear) The Reaper" is the smash single gift that keeps on giving.

August 6 – 24, 1978. Amidst the band's usual (but unusual in the industry, at least to this extent) greatly varied billings, a leg of the US tour sees BÖC supported by UFO and British Lions, an offshoot band from Mott the Hoople.

Late September 1978. Columbia issue a second BÖC live album, although not a double but a single, called *Some Enchanted Evening*. It becomes the band's best-selling album of all time, reaching #44 on Billboard. The chief single is a cover of The Animals' "We Gotta Get Out of This Place" backed with "E.T.I. (Live)." In the UK, the B-side is "Stairway to the Stars". In Germany, it's the band's cover of the MC5's "Kick Out the Jams."

October 2, 1978. *Mommie Dearest*, Christina Crawford's memoir of life with her difficult mother Joan Crawford, is published, through William Morrow & Co. Three years later it would be turned into a notorious movie. Also in 1981, Blue Öyster Cult would score an underground hit with their song, "Joan Crawford".

November 10, 1978. Epic/CBS issues *Give 'Em Enough Rope*, by The Clash. It is infamously produced by BÖC manager Sandy Pearlman who is said to have brought to the band a bit too much heavy metal polish.

June 2, 1978,
De Montfort Hall, Leicester.

Set-list:
R. U. Ready to Rock
ETI
Harvester Of Eyes
Cities On Flame
We Gotta Get Outta This Place
Golden Age Of Leather
Astronomy
ME262
Hot Rails To Hell
Godzilla
This Ain´t the Summer Of Love
5 Guitar Medley
Born To Be Wild
(Don't Fear) The Reaper

© Alan Perry Concert Photography

June 2, 1978,
De Montfort Hall, Leicester.

© Alan Perry Concert Photography

June 2, 1978, De Montfort Hall, Leicester.

June 2, 1978, De Montfort Hall, Leicester.

BLUE OYSTER CULT

Oyster Cult back for more

BLUE OYSTER CULT will play a second series of British dates following their previously announced tour at the end of this month.

Such has been the demand for tickets that the band will return to Britain at the end of May following their European tour for six more concerts.

They start at Liverpool Empire May 30 and then play Edinburgh Odeon 31, Newcastle City Hall June 1, Leicester De Montfort Hall (moved from the original date on April 26) 2, Bournemouth Winter Gardens 3, London Hammersmith Odeon 4.

This makes three London concerts and two Newcastle concerts for the group who will be bringing with them what is claimed to be the most extensive laser show ever presented.

© Alan Perry Concert Photography

June 2, 1978, De Montfort Hall, Leicester.

June 2, 1978, De Montfort Hall, Leicester.

Blue Oyster Cult
Bristol

FLAMING PYROTECHNICS, lasers, smoke . . . plus great rock'n'roll; Blue Oyster Cult is the group you always dreamt about. Even though there were sound problems and the visual effects had to be curtailed somewhat, this first date of their UK tour proved that this is one band who have no trouble living up to their semi-mythical status.

Main vocalist is Eric Bloom, who plays guitar too but takes time out to stalk the stage like a Manson/biker mutation, all leather-coated growls'n'howls. The band's line-up has always seemed a bit anonymous on records, but onstage it's easier to enjoy the individual personalities: Allen Lanier doing his guitarings and Phantom Of The Opera keyboard-hunch, Donald 'Buck Dharma' Roeser on stripy suit and six-string magic, A. and J. Bouchard on drums and bass respectively (sturdy boys indeed).

They opened with 'R.U. Ready 2 Rock' from the recent 'Spectres' album and then whomped into 'E.T.I. (Extra Terrestrial Intelligence)' from 'Agents Of Fortune', the previous record. Those two albums are generally considered to be more 'poppy' than the other four they've done, but in a live situation the unity of all their songs comes through: this stuff blends perfectly with the (supposedly) harsher tones of 'Harvester Of Eyes' and 'Cities On Flame' (on which drummer-boy Albert takes lead vocals), where Bloom gets to beat a mean cymbal.

The lasers and all that techo-hardware are used sparingly and effectively, not just as gratuitous embellishment. Sometimes they have a single beam trained on one of those revolving ballroom-globe things, splashing stars across the audience; at others interweaving lines dance across the ceiling through the smoke, the full-scale stuff coming in during 'Godzilla' (their tribute to Japanese culture) while Albert dons a horse's head (Patti!?) for a synth-treated drum solo on a Doors/'Texas Radio And The Big Beat' level.

They also showed their Animal-istic side by doing 'We Gotta Get Outta This Place', which'll be included on a forthcoming live elpee, and the Stones get a nod during Joe's bass solo in 'This Ain't The Summer Of Love', when he slips in the riff of 'Why Don't We Sing This Song All Together' from 'Satanic Majesties . . .'. That leads into the famous bit where the *whole band* plays axes, followed by their famed 'Born To Be Wild' interpretation (let's hear it for Mars Bonfire!) where Buck and Bloom indulge in some guitar *frottage* . . . wonderful and enriching life experiences every one.

Gawd, and they encored with *the hit single* '(Don't Fear) The

BLUE OYSTER CULT: wonderful and enriching

BLUE OYSTER CULT: eardrum wrenching

And the road goes on forever

BLUE ÖYSTER CULT 'Some Enchanted Evening' (CBS 86074)★★★★

IT COULD have ended my favored shout, but right now I'm away with Sandy Pearlman (with odd bits of Carl behind the desk) yet again, ragingly as all the sonic young bloods of BÖC cut tributes to themselves from mythic cosmologies and roll mythology and meaty real-world rock real.

BÖC (typical style, made thicker for the recap) made it weird HM double (even in-around the studio raves with pretty kitty cats), with two pretty kitty cats with two pretty distinctly friendly players; which is deeply disturbing with no solid rock relief; with a side of 'Agents Of Fortune' action 'Spectres'). The former gave

them a hit in '(Don't Fear) The Reaper' and the latter consolidated the cult, the mobile rising the cult followed that one of the solid aura of 'kill us all kind of-all-out to kill us in kindness' (Which if note — G.C.)

What the band has done here is to take raw ideas (they being of the genuinely the time being) of the album, and fibrous pieces of BÖC credibility and transform their own a bit in a slowdown that jumps skewing at time but then power still on there.

What you get is a rakishly culled (to prove they can still cheek) tribute to their original feeling on the live cuts contains the famous cuts (here, each two cover versions, and seven favourite to keep a ties with

their past), Production and performance are both fine enough to give the feel of moments of the six 'R' Or On You Are On Your Feet package, but there were songs are always the band's best wrenchin' Is to as central as any of the staff of the first album or 'Tyranny and Mutation' and the cuts here Rock 'n' Roll' (R.U. Ready 2 Tyrantin') and 'E.T.I. (Extra Terrestrial Intelligence) are the best mesh the colour the bit and best repeat of years.

The cover versions are masterful, the 'Kick Out The Jams' smashes the cadaveric the MC5 kick cadaveric of the Hot Tuna's vol, but I can just off it's more the easy way and record better the song's original the larger egos here, surely. You Get Outta' Walk The Animals Of Ty just suberbly of the Animals Of Ty hype her hinny and silbery Jat and the jazzing and bacious battery each, echo of earthshaky such forth.

Conceivably a few have come to include my stake in the top of (if) rather roots of the identity of an artistically yet all ad (if) rather "the Harmony" from the 'rent Treatise' album has always been a favorite song. It's a way too strikinging of my stake, and I'll to stand here stretched on an end of sensing for myself, with well though, it's a killer. In fact I hink it may include a second kiss to so show of contact of Blue Öyster Cult, provide just of its of style of the material and quite other than Blue Öyster Cult, of the material and quality of proving songs also sig- to make Blue Öyster Cult's not this that songs also sig- to make blue albums too. Also of those albums too. Also on the road of the albums.

BÖC ON TOUR FOREVER. **SANDY ROBERTSON**

SOME ENCHANTED EVENING YOU WILL MEET THE REAPER

A LIVE EXPLOSION FROM THE BLUE ÖYSTER CULT

'Some Enchanted Evening' — a live recording of highlights from the Blue Öyster Cult 1978 tour from the City Hall, Newcastle, to the Fox Theatre, Atlanta.
'Some Enchanted Evening' features electrifying live versions of 'R.U. Ready 2 Rock', 'Kick Out The Jams', and 'Don't Fear The Reaper'

Blue Öyster Cult/Live Album/'Some Enchanted Evening'. Cassette/8 track.

Page 30 SOUNDS May 13, 1978 — May 13, 1978 SOUNDS Page 31

B·L·U·E O·Y·S·T·E·R C·U·L·T

SANDY ROBERTSON RAPS COSMICALLY WITH GUITARIST ERIC BLOOM AND MENTOR/PRODUCER SANDY PEARLMAN

ERIC BLOOM: 'The new wave is a crock of shit'

SANDY PEARLMAN and bedtime reading: 'I'm always dreaming'

CONTINUED PAGE 34

P E A R L M A N

FROM PAGE 31

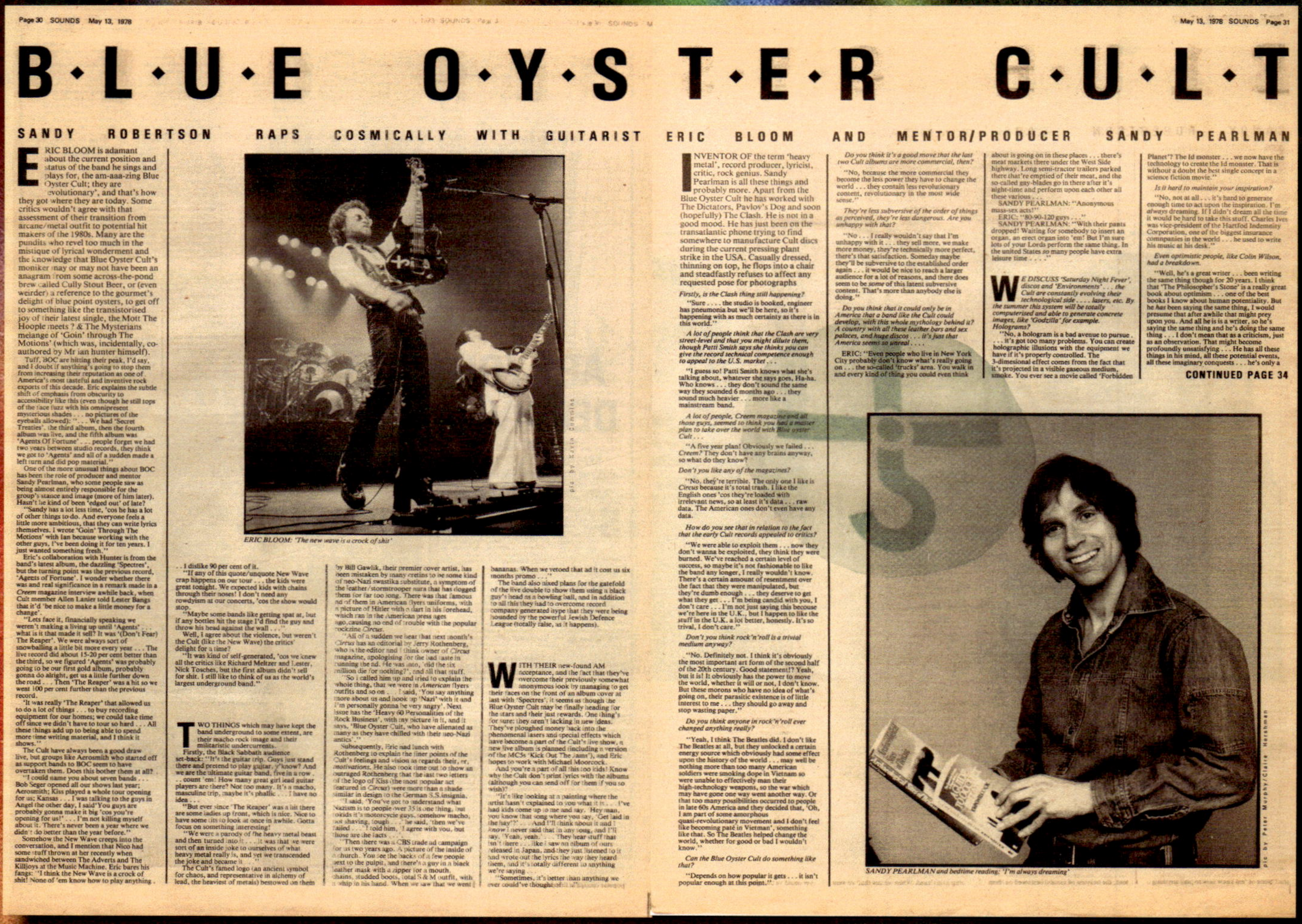

Memorabilia, Jim Powell Collection

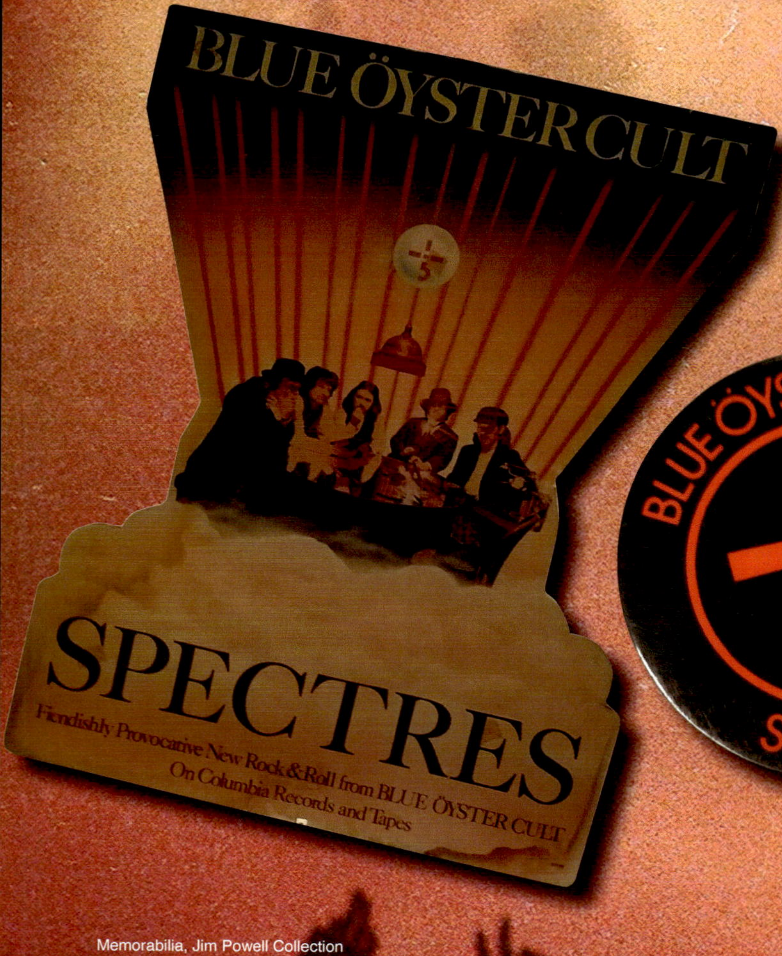

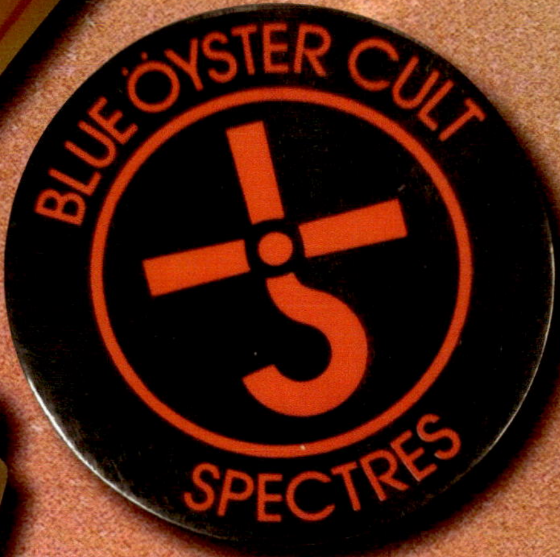

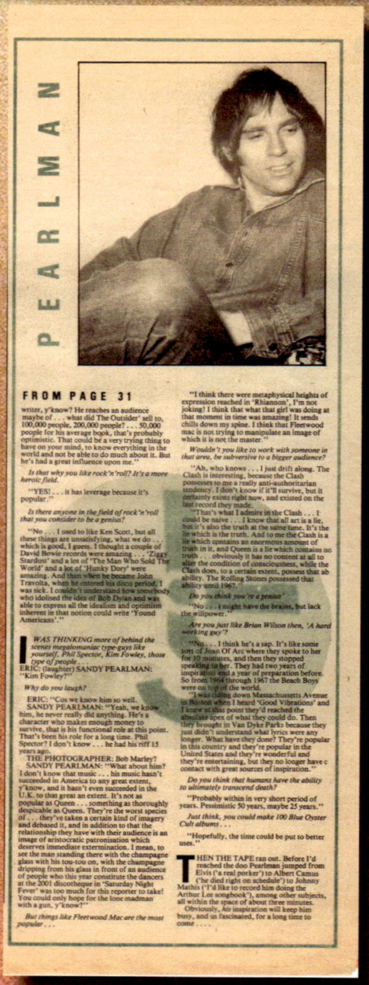

June 2, 1978,
De Montfort Hall, Leicester.

Kansas on Blue Öyster Cult's stage.

© Rich Galbraith

September 2, 1978, Day On The Green, Oakland Stadium, Oakland, California.

© Daniel Larsen / Frank White Photo Agency

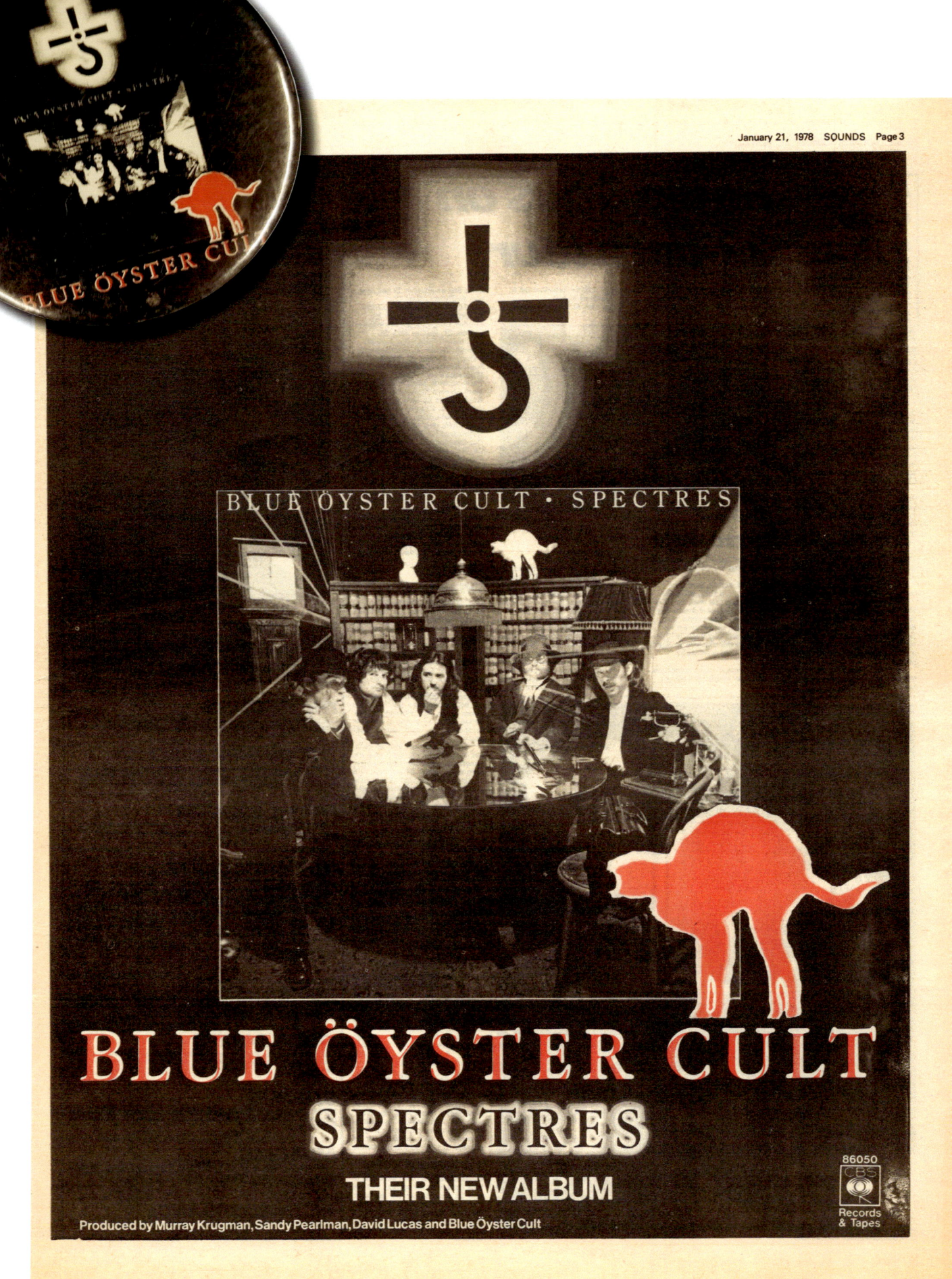

1979

1979. The Karl G. Jansky Very Large Array (VLA), nears completion after six years of work. The configuration of twenty-seven dishes in the New Mexico desert is designed to catch radio signals from space, most intriguingly and hopefully, from intelligent alien life. BÖC song "The Vigil" contains the line, "27 faces, with their eyes turned to the sky," in homage.

February 11, 1979. The infamous Ayatollah Khomeini, an Islamic revivalist, rises to power in Iran. Donald is inspired to write a song about the event for his solo album, entitled "Divine Wind".

March 1979. The band work with producer Tom Werman in California, on songs to appear on their forthcoming sixth record. Amidst the sessions, they perform club dates as Soft White Underbelly.

April 1979. Ted Nugent joins the band onstage for a performance of "Roadhouse Blues".

May 6 – 10, 1979. The band play their first dates ever in Japan.

May 13, 1979. On the way back from Japan, BÖC play two shows in Hawaii, the second of which marks the last use of the band's cumbersome and temperamental laser light show.

June 1, 1979. John Shirley sees publication of his first novel *Transmaniacon*. The book is rife with Blue Öyster Cult references. Shirley would go on to pen many of the lyrics on BÖC albums *Heaven Forbid* and *Curse of the Hidden Mirror*.

June 19, 1979. Columbia issue a sixth BÖC studio album, called *Mirrors*. Disappointingly, after a string of certifications for the band, the album fails to reach gold. It is called too pop, with much of the blame falling upon producer Tom Werman, who in fact gives the band its most high-fidelity production job yet. The album reaches #44 on Billboard and #46 in the UK charts.

July 19, 1979. The band play an unscheduled pick-up date at the Mid-Hudson Civic Center in Poughkeepsie, NY, supported by The Lisa Hartman Band and Roadmaster. It's the first BÖC concert for the author of this book, 16 years old at the time, clear across the country from his home in British Columbia on an epic driving summer vacation in the family camper van.

August 1979. "Mirrors"/"Lonely Teardrops" is issued as a single, but only in the UK. Japan issues "Moon Crazy" as a single, backed with "I Am the Storm".

September 1979. The most widely available single from *Mirrors* is "In Thee" (a rare Allen Lanier composition) backed with "Lonely Teardrops." The track reaches #74 on the Billboard charts.

October 1979. The UK issues "In Thee" as a single but chooses "The Vigil" for its B-side.

Late 1979. The second and last US single from *Mirrors* is "You're Not the One (I Was Looking For)" backed with "Moon Crazy". The A-side is a pop song written by Albert Bouchard, who wrote it as a joke parody of The Cars' "Just What I Needed." Bouchard was shocked that the song was picked for inclusion on the record. Albert's soon to be estranged wife Caryn gets a lyric credit.

November 1 – 13, 1979. The band conduct their second UK tour, supported by prog rockers Magnum.

February 16, 1979,
Benefit Show, Palladium,
New York City.

© John T Comerford / Frank White Photo Agency

February 16, 1979,
Benefit Show, Palladium,
New York City.

Memorabilia, Jim Powell Collection

August 19, 1979,
Spartan Stadium,
San Jose, California.

August 19, 1979,
Spartan Stadium,
San Jose, California.

© Daniel Larsen / Frank White Photo Agency

August 19, 1979,
Spartan Stadium,
San Jose, California.

Japan Tour programme 1979.

UK Tour programme 1979.

Photo: Joe Bouchard Collection

"Cultösaurus Erectus *was an obvious return to scary sounds. I remember myself lobbying very hard to not make a commercial record, not worrying about it, just getting back to writing those weird songs again. That's when we thought, we've turned off all these people, and we have to get them turned on again. We have to show them that our hearts are pure and that we're going to stick with our image and that we can do a scary mysterioso, and just be odd and quirky, make the kind of music that would make you think. And I guess after the disaster that was* Mirrors, *one of the first steps was getting somebody heavier in to produce."*
Albert Bouchard

THE 1980s

July 4, 1980,
Day On The Green,
Oakland Stadium,
Oakland, California.

With these bands — and then with all these books I do on them — I can't help but analyze their careers against two hard rock phenomena of the '80s, first, the New Wave of British Heavy Metal, and second, the hair metal era spanning roughly 1983 to 1991. As it turns out, Blue Öyster Cult would participate somewhat in the former, gamely reflecting new heavy realities and then playing the UK properly, but then, alas, completely pooch it on the latter, missing out fantastically on something that could have been a second victory lap in a sort of five-year span.

So our heroes enter the decade hell-bent on making a fairly heavy, underground album to reverse the poor opinions showered down upon them because of *Mirrors*, specifically the likes of "In Thee" and "You're Not the One (I Was Looking For)." But let's face it: *Cultösaurus Erectus* is not that much of an about-face from *Mirrors*. Sure, it's somewhat heavier, but this symbolic move from Tom Werman to Martin Birch didn't mean a heck of a lot in the long run, and it sure didn't bring them any more success.

The band's 1980 album did about the same kind of business as *Mirrors*, but the band could indeed satisfy themselves that they had a bit of a recovery in terms of their reputation. Fortunately, the blue period — I always equate these two records with ZZ Top's *El Loco* for some reason — was about to end with *Fire of Unknown Origin*, which would mark a sprightly and energetic second wind for the band.

Led by the tight, updated pop of "Burnin' for You" but then bolstered by the likes of "Veteran of the Psychic Wars", "Vengeance (The Pact)" and most notable among the second-stringers, "Joan Crawford", *Fire of Unknown Origin* would represent this band's *Heaven and Hell*, rather than their *Mob Rules*. In other words, with Martin Birch producing in 1980 and 1981 a pair of Black Sabbath albums and a pair of Blue Öyster Cult albums, the Sabs did the best with the first of theirs while Blue Öyster Cult did the best with the second one.

Also, interestingly enough, both bands — and as discussed in the timeline, both managed at this point by Sandy Pearlman — would follow up with double live albums not particularly well received by their fan bases. Similarly, both bands' fortunes would degrade dramatically over the course of the eighties as memberships weakened and the records started sounding strange.

But back on topic, we're talking about the Cultsters here. Moving on past *Extraterrestrial Live*, BÖC had lost one of their original members and key writers in Albert Bouchard, and we were on our way to *The Revolution by Night*, a record marred by the worst excesses of eighties production values. Whereas the previous album was gold and well on the way to platinum (never officially designated so, much to the annoyance of the band who think it's past a million, as do I), *The Revolution by Night* stalled below gold, just like *Mirrors* and *Cultösaurus Erectus*.

It would be two years before the next record. The pricey and poppy *Club Ninja* would demonstrate that the band had lost the plot. Wayward, uninspired, song-doctored and awkward… no one liked the damn thing, although long-time fans appreciated "Perfect Water" as sufficiently creative and "Dancing in the Ruins" as a pop song at least 40% as good as "Burnin' for You".

But don't forget, it's 1986 into 1987, and melodic, poppy hard rock with great guitar playing is huge in America. And here we have BÖC fantastically going in the wrong direction whilst their contemporaries…

okay, many failed the same, but Kiss figured it out and Aerosmith *killed* it. Heart killed it too. And Alice Cooper, who was even older than BÖC (his hit records were past him just as BÖC was ascending), he figured it out too.

But yeah, by this point the band had been bounced hard out of the hockey arenas and into clubs and theatres. Their proposal for 1988, *Imaginos*, a dog's breakfast of an album featuring a bewildering number of guests over years of expensive sessions, wouldn't aid the cause. And forget hair metal; this should've been the band's crowning glory because of the long-discussed bringing to fruition of a complete telling of the *Imaginos* saga.

But this tends to happen, doesn't it? The fans that were falling over themselves wanting Dio to do a concept album and Rush to do a concept album, when *Magica* and *Clockwork Angels* came along, both bands' bases were vaguely unsatisfied (actually, a qualification, with Rush, fans were loving it initially but the bloom has worn off hard). As well, Iron Maiden didn't exactly set the world on fire with *Seventh Son of a Seventh Son*, and Black Sabbath certainly didn't capture fans' imaginations with *Tyr*, which, granted, is a half-hearted attempt at concept.

No, as Albert lamented — and this is the long-exiled Albert at this point, toiling away on the *Imaginos* concept on his own, with periodic prodding from Sandy —
Imaginos should've been a double album, made in a proper continuous recording session by the original band. Instead, it's a hodgepodge of different productions, random access sequencing, and in the end, it was simply wrong that it was a single record. As a result, it faded into the woodwork as quickly as *Club Ninja* did.

So yeah, the story of the eighties, which you are about to experience in eye-frying detail, at least in terms of the hard facts, is one of maintenance then a bit of a slingshot effect and then a little more maintenance through the early eighties, with the band still cruising along and paying the bills.

However, pretty much at the time, ears stop ringing at the close of the *Revolution by Night* touring cycle, the band experience a quick drop into personnel changes, the occasional hiatus and two flawed records, records flawed in two totally different ways, which, through the performance art of the dual flawing, demonstrate that this band really could flaw good when they put their minds to it.

July 4, 1980,
Day On The Green,
Oakland Stadium,
Oakland, California.

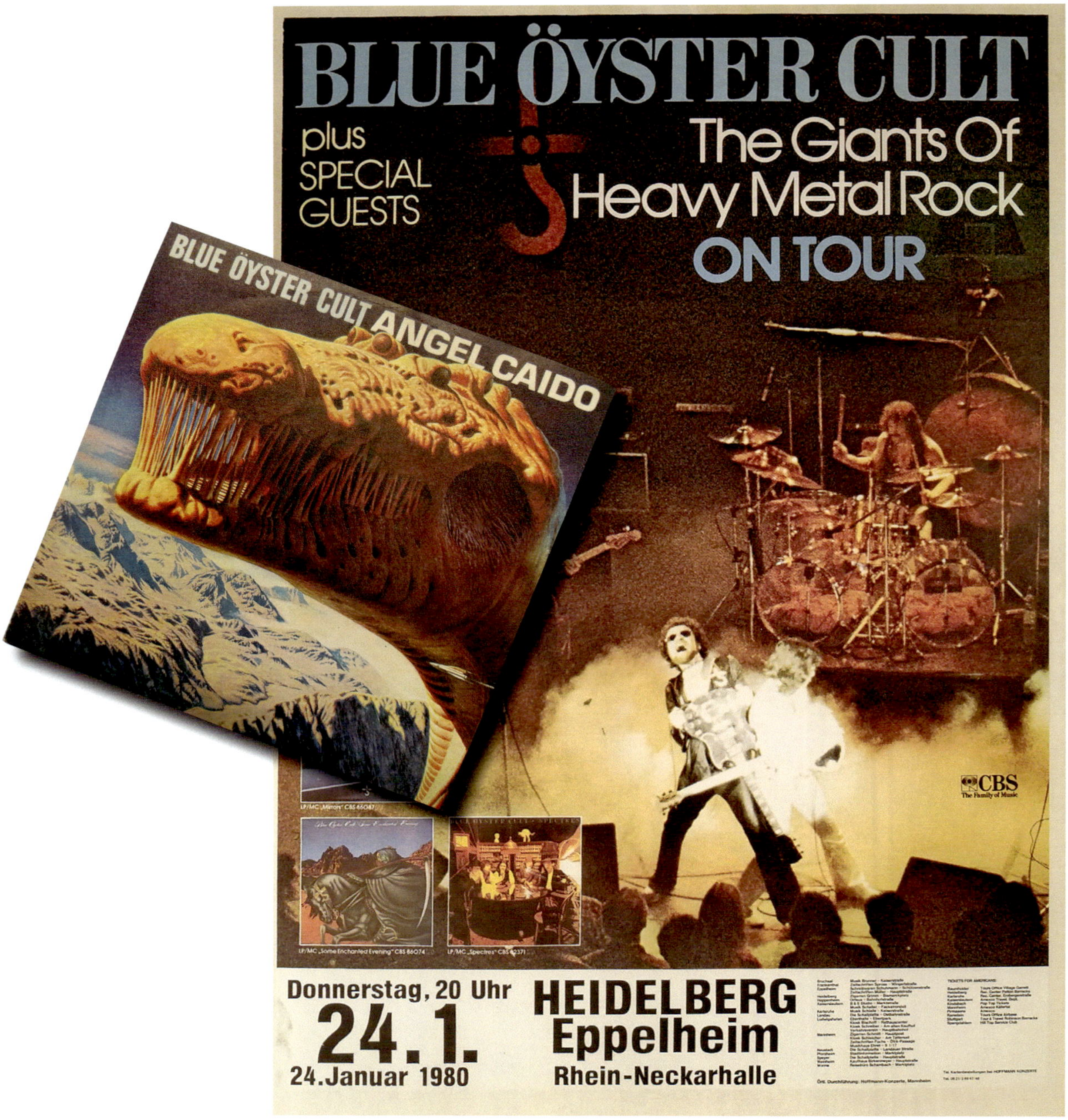
BLUE ÖYSTER CULT
plus SPECIAL GUESTS
The Giants Of Heavy Metal Rock
ON TOUR
CBS The Family of Music
LP/MC „Mirrors" CBS 86087
LP/MC „Some Enchanted Evening" CBS 86074
LP/MC „Spectres" CBS 82371
Donnerstag, 20 Uhr
24.1.
24.Januar 1980
HEIDELBERG
Eppelheim
Rhein-Neckarhalle
BLUE ÖYSTER CULT ANGEL CAIDO

A NEW MONSTER ALBUM
BLUE ÖYSTER CULT
CULTÖSAURUS ERECTUS
"LP"
Hear the album between 12 & 2 p.m. Thursday 10th July – 17th July and get the album at least £1 off our R.R.P. at the following dealers.
STARRING
ERIC BLOOM
DONALD (BUCK DHARMA) ROESER
ALLEN LANIER
JOE BOUCHARD
ALBERT BOUCHARD
FEATURING
'THE MARSHALL PLAN'
'FALLEN ANGEL'
'MONSTERS'
'LIPS IN THE HILLS'
PRODUCER
MARTIN BIRCH
DIRECTOR
SANDY PEARLMAN
RECORDED ON LOCATION IN LONG ISLAND, N.Y.
GET THIS MONSTER BEFORE IT GETS YOU!
NOT FOR PERSONS OF NERVOUS DISPOSITION
Page 46 — New Musical Express

BLUE ÖYSTER CULT
CULTÖSAURUS ERECTUS

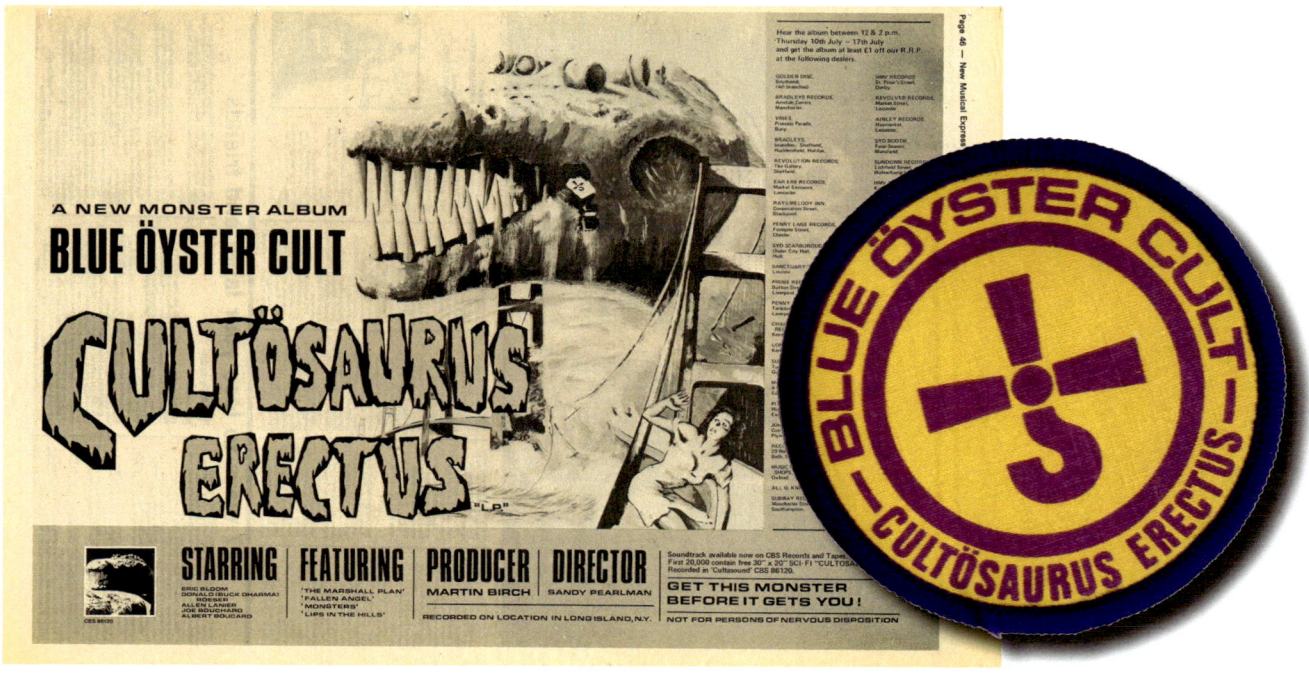

1980

January 3, 1980. New York poet Jim Carroll sees the release of his debut album, *Catholic Boy*, on Atco. Allen Lanier co-writes one track and plays keys on two. Carroll would pen the lyrics to "Perfect Water" on BÖC album *Club Ninja*.

February 7, 1980. Future Blue Öyster Cult engineer and bassist Richie Castellano is born, in Brooklyn, NY.

Spring 1980. The band work at Kingdom Sound Studios in Long Island, NY on what will be their seventh album.

June 14, 1980. Columbia issues the band's seventh studio album, the Martin Birch-produced *Cultösaurus Erectus*. Albert says that the band was attempting to get back to their tougher and more "mysterioso" roots. Deep Purple veteran Birch had just come off of producing Black Sabbath's *Heaven and Hell* and Whitesnake's *Ready an' Willing*. The debut single in the US — non-picture sleeve — is the re-monikered "Here's Johnny (The Marshall Plan)"/"Divine Wind," which does nothing.

June 18 – 22, 1980. The band play three *Cultösaurus* tour warm-up shows in New York as Soft White Underbelly.

July 3, 1980. *Some Enchanted Evening* achieves its US gold certification.

July 13 – October 25, 1980. The band conduct their infamous Black & Blue co-headlining tour of the US with Black Sabbath, over the course of which tensions rose between both bands' crews and then some of the band members themselves. In the middle was Sandy Pearlman, manager of both bands. Many acts support along the way, including Molly Hatchet, Sammy Hagar and Riot. Regular support comes from French act Shakin' Street, who are also managed by Sandy and feature Ross the Boss of Dictators fame on guitar.

July 30 – August 7, 1980. Future manager Steve Schenck sits in on keys for an ailing Allen.

September 8, 1980. A gig that the band performs at the Old Waldorf in San Francisco is broadcast live by KSAN.

October 1980. CBS in the UK goes with "Deadline"/"Monsters" as the single from *Cultösaurus Erectus*, another spot of wishful thinking. They also try "Fallen Angel"/"Lips in the Hills," which is more hopeful, but still does little business.

October 9, 1980. A Black & Blue tour date in Milwaukee results in a riot when Black Sabbath leaves the stage two songs in after Geezer Butler gets hit with a bottle. The crowd of 9,000 had already become restless after a fifty-five-minute wait between the end of BÖC's set and the start of Sabbath's, with long set-ups and tear-downs being one of the perennial aggravations on this tour. More than 160 people are arrested. A less severe riot takes place two weeks earlier in Willkes-Barre, Pennsylvania, resulting in the arrest of Steve Schenck.

October 17, 1980. A Black & Blue show in Nassau is taped and released as a VHS video.

December 6, 1980. BÖC appear on Don Kirshner's Rock Concert (Season 8, Episode 13), performing "Born to Be Wild". Also aired is concert footage of "Godzilla" and the video clip for "The Marshall Plan" which, on the just released *Cultösaurus Erectus* album, includes a cameo speaking part by Kirshner himself.

Photo: Joe Bouchard Collection

Memorabilia, Jim Powell Collection

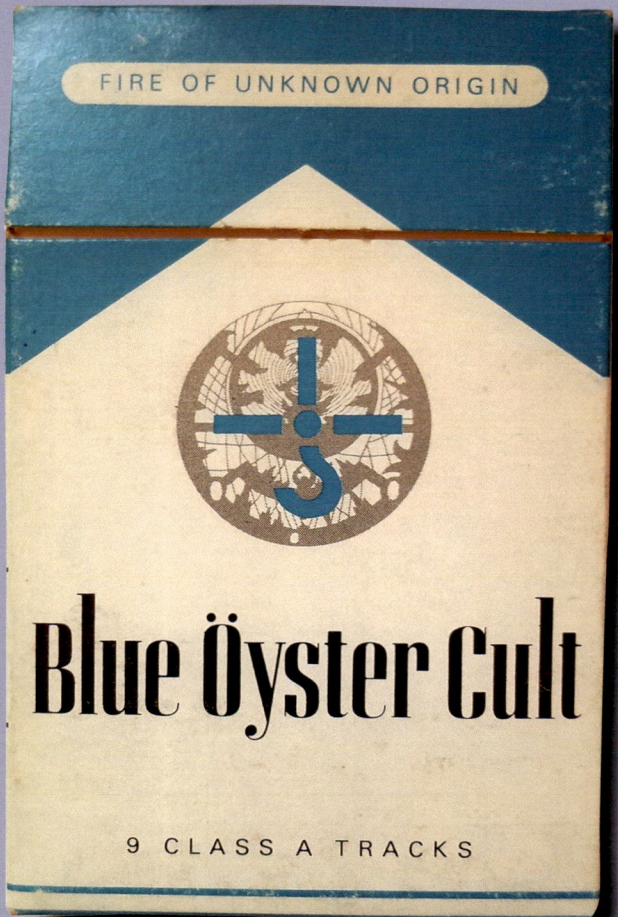
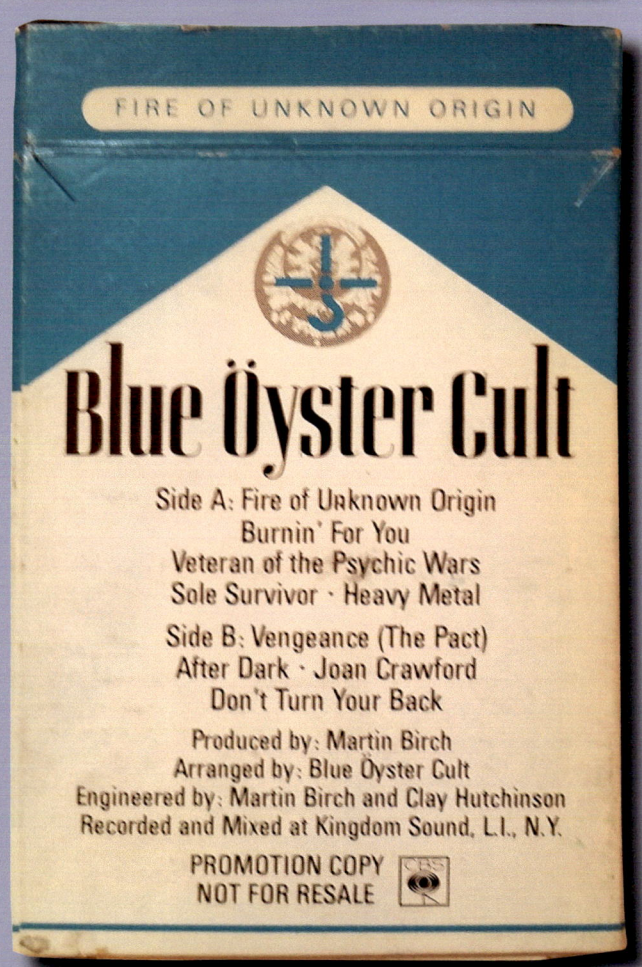

Memorabilia, Jim Powell Collection

July 4, 1981, Day On The Green, Oakland Stadium, Oakland, California.

© Daniel Larsen / Frank White Photo Agency

1981

1981. Columbia, under their Collectables imprint, float a single in the US pairing "(Don't Fear) The Reaper" with "Burnin' for You". Little did they know that this would constitute the biggest couple of hits the band would ever have, together on one tidy 45.

February 3, 1981. Rainbow issue *Difficult to Cure*, featuring future BÖC drummer Bobby Rondinelli, who also plays on the follow-up record, *Straight Between the Eyes*. Rainbow's last album (before reunion), 1983's *Bent Out of Shape*, also features a future Cultster on drums, Chuck Bürgi.

June 12 – June 16, 1981. As was the case with the previous record cycle, the band do a few club dates as Soft White Underbelly to warm up for their next major campaign. Support comes from Jim Carroll and David Roter (as David Roter Method), both contributors of lyrics to BÖC songs.

June 19, 1981. The summer of 1981 sees not only the arrival of MTV, but also the eighth Blue Öyster Cult album, *Fire of Unknown Origin*, which, like its predecessor, is produced by Martin Birch, who also does a second Black Sabbath album the same year. The cover art is by Greg Scott, who begins a productive and memorable few years with the band. "Burnin' for You" is issued as the album's only single, but in many permutations and in many territories. At this point the New Wave of British Heavy Metal is in full swing and the band is well regarded by hard rock fans, given the relative riffiness of this record and its predecessor, *Cultösaurus Erectus*.

June 24 – August 11, 1981. The band perform concert dates to promote *Fire of Unknown Origin*, this first leg consisting of North American dates supported in the main by Pat Travers Band, Johnny Van Zant, UFO and Humble Pie. Along the way are a Day on the Green show, Oregon Jam and the 1000 Islands Festival where they play with Chubby Checker. Steve Schenk is also called upon to tinkle the keys on occasion and Ray Manzarek guests at an LA show on July 26th.

July 11, 1981. The author fishes a one-dollar bill out of his pocket in the hotel elevator on the way to the band's gig at the local hockey barn in Spokane, Washington. Eric Bloom obliges and signs it in pencil.

August 7, 1981. Animated fantasy movie *Heavy Metal* hits theatres. The film is based on the French fantasy magazine of the same name. The hit double LP soundtrack album features tracks mostly from hard rock bands, including BÖC, who are on board with "Veteran of the Psychic Wars". The band wrote "Vengeance (The Pact)" specifically for the movie but it was rejected because it was too close to a plot summary, specifically the "Taarna's Theme" segment. Also written for the movie — according to Albert, BÖC were to dominate with five to seven tracks — were "Don't Turn Your Back" and "Heavy Metal: The Black and Silver". All four songs appear on *Fire of Unknown Origin* but only one made the soundtrack album. Sandy's other charges, Black Sabbath, are also involved in the *Heavy Metal* project, represented on the soundtrack album with a version of "The Mob Rules" that was recorded before the version used on the album *Mob Rules*.

August 18, 1981. Senior crew member Rick Downey is called upon to drum on four songs at a show at the West Runton Pavilion in England because Albert Bouchard shows up late for the gig.

August 20, 1981. Albert performs his last concert with the band (other than a handful of dates over the ensuing decades), after showing up late for a second gig in a couple days. He is fired that night. Albert had been lodging separate from the band, with a lady friend who was not his wife, which had the band wives up in arms and calling for Albert's head. Exiled, Bouchard begins thinking even more about Sandy's long gestating *Imaginos* song and story cycle and secures, with

July 4, 1981, Day On The Green, Oakland Stadium, Oakland, California.

Sandy, an advance from Columbia to begin work on the project, which would be assembled in fits and starts over the next seven years.

August 22, 1981. Downey plays his first big show with the band and it's huge — Donington Monsters of Rock, in front of an estimated crowd of 60,000. Brutal PA issues wreck Slade's set and then BÖC's as well. The band slink off the stage with the biggest defeat of their concert career.

August 30, 1981. The band play a one-off show in Hawaii, along with Heart, Gamma and Fortune.

September 2 – December 31, 1981. BÖC conduct a second intensive US tour leg in support of *Fire of Unknown Origin*. Support on most shows comes from Foghat and Whitford St. Holmes.

September 18, 1981. Docudrama *Mommie Dearest*, based on the book of the same name about the life of Joan Crawford, is issued. The film stars Faye Dunaway.

October 6, 1981. Egyptian President Anwar Sadat is assassinated. Buck, a great admirer of Sadat, writes an instrumental called "Anwar's Theme" that appears on his solo album the following year.

December 15, 1981. The Doors' Robbie Krieger joins the band on stage during a performance of "Roadhouse Blues" at The Country Club in Reseda, CA, following up a cameo earlier on the tour in Chicago. The show is videotaped for satellite broadcast. This version of "Roadhouse Blues" shows up on the band's ensuing live album, *Extraterrestrial Live*.

July 4 1981, Day On The Green, Oakland Stadium, Oakland, California.

September 18, 1981, Madison Square Garden, New York City.

September 18, 1981, Madison Square Garden, New York City.

September 18, 1981,
Madison Square Garden,
New York City.

December 26, 1981, Capitol Theatre, Passaic, New Jersey.

December 26, 1981, Capitol Theatre, Passaic, New Jersey.

December 26, 1981, Capitol Theatre, Passaic, New Jersey.

© Frank White Photo Agency

December 26, 1981,
Capitol Theatre, Passaic, New Jersey.

December 30, 1981, Nassau Veterans Memorial Coliseum, Uniondale, New York.

1982

January 1982. Utopia's Kasim Sulton issues a solo album on EMI called *Kasim*. Buck provides guitar solos for three tracks. The producer on board is Vancouver's Bruce Fairbairn, who will produce the next BÖC album. Kasim will join BÖC in 2012.

January – June 1982. The band is inactive as Buck works on his solo album and Columbia readies a BÖC live album.

Late March 1982. Capitol issues *Illuminations*, a double album from a Canadian progressive rock band Leggat. Opening track "White Flags" would be covered by BÖC on *Club Ninja*.

March 27, 1982. Columbia issue a third BÖC live album, a double, called *Extraterrestrial Live*. Greg Scott returns as the band's cover artist, turning in one of his classy monochromatic illustrations.

April 1, 1982. *Fire of Unknown Origin* is certified gold in Canada.

June 1982. "Burnin' for You"/"(Don't Fear) The Reaper" is issued as a single from the recent BÖC live album.

June 15, 1982. Donald issues a buoyant and poppy solo album called *Flat Out*, featuring a bevy of studio musicians and guests. Two singles are issued, namely "Born to Rock" and "Your Loving Heart."

June 20, 1982, L'Amour Brooklyn, New York.

June 20, 1982, L'Amour, Brooklyn, New York.

June 17 – December 29, 1982. The band tour the US and Canada, promoting their third live album. They are supported in the main by Aldo Nova, a Canadian artist also on CBS, specifically Portrait, a subsidiary. The previous month, his debut album had just gone platinum in the US. Aldo Nova would co-write "Take Me Away" which was to become the biggest hit from Blue Öyster Cult's next studio album, issued in 1983.

September 1982. John Cale's eight studio album *Music for a New Society* features Allen Lanier on guitar.

November 19, 1982. *Fire of Unknown Origin* receives its RIAA gold certification, driven by big crowds for the co-headlining touring with Black Sabbath, as well as the considerable success of "Burnin' for You" as a single.

June 20, 1982, L'Amour, Brooklyn, New York.

© Frank White Photo Agency

June 20, 1982, L'Amour, Brooklyn, New York.

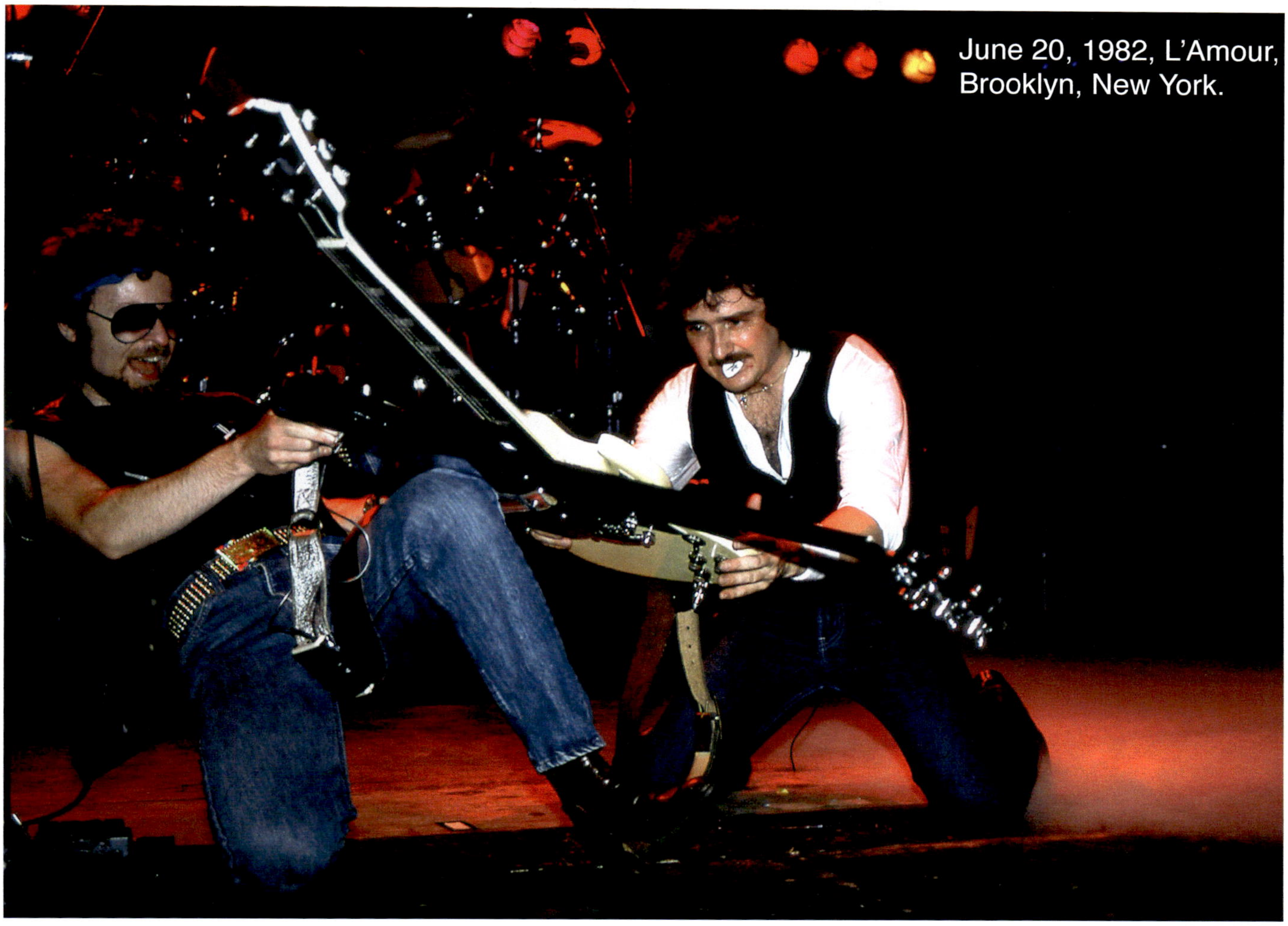

June 20, 1982, L'Amour, Brooklyn, New York.

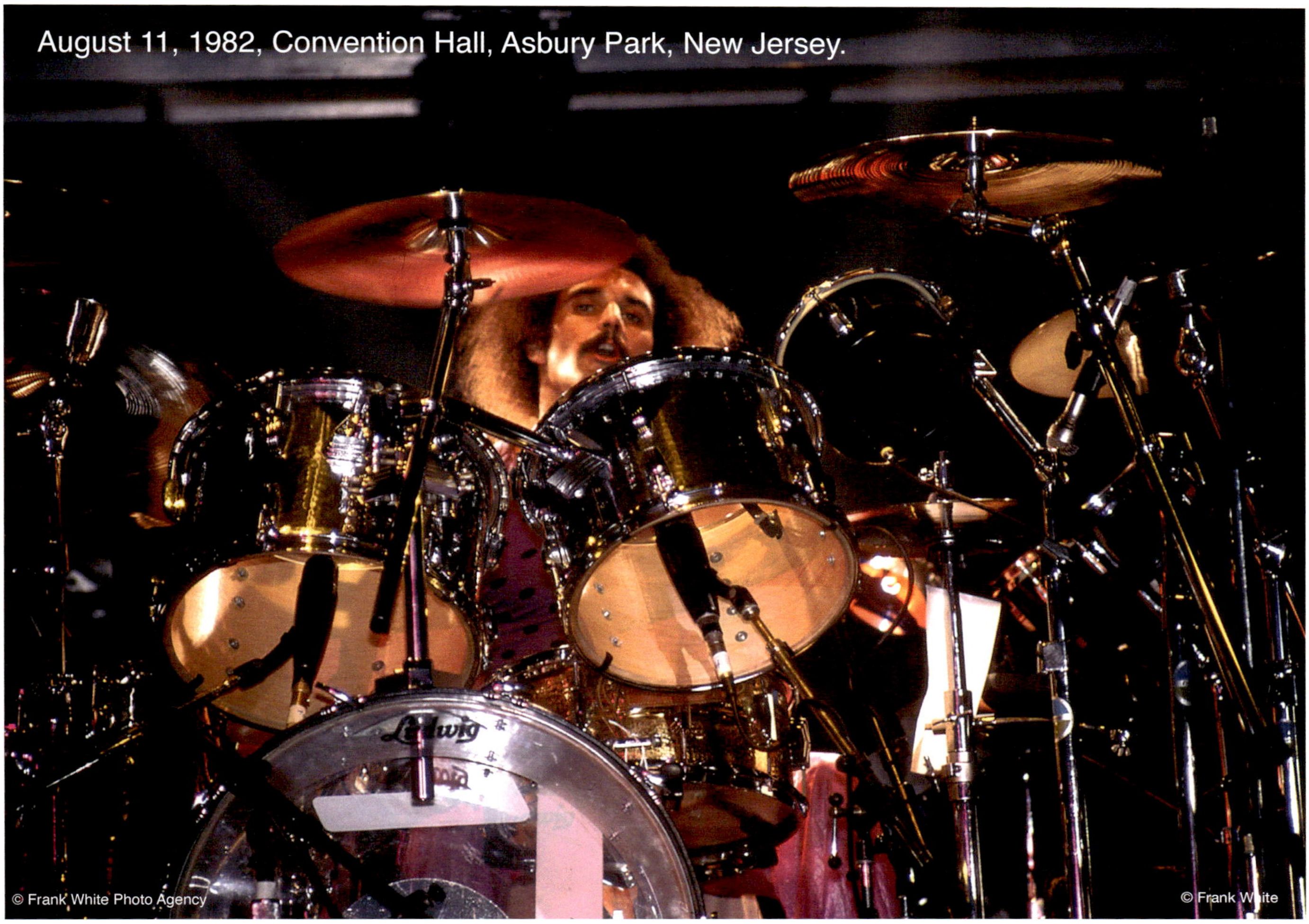

August 11, 1982, Convention Hall, Asbury Park, New Jersey.

© Frank White Photo Agency

© Frank White

© Frank White

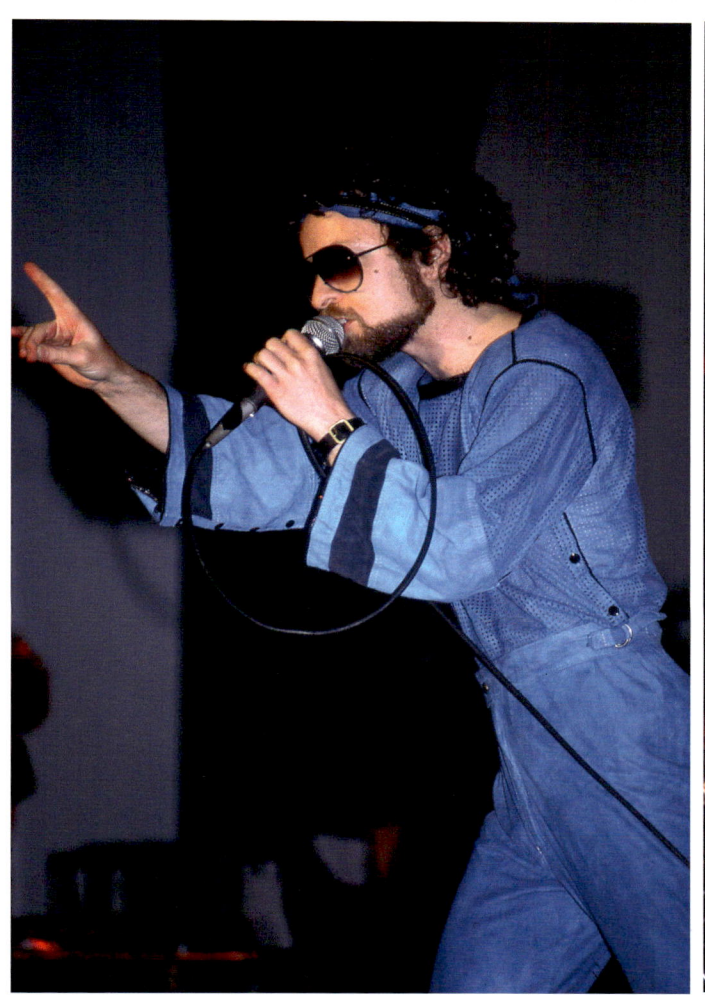

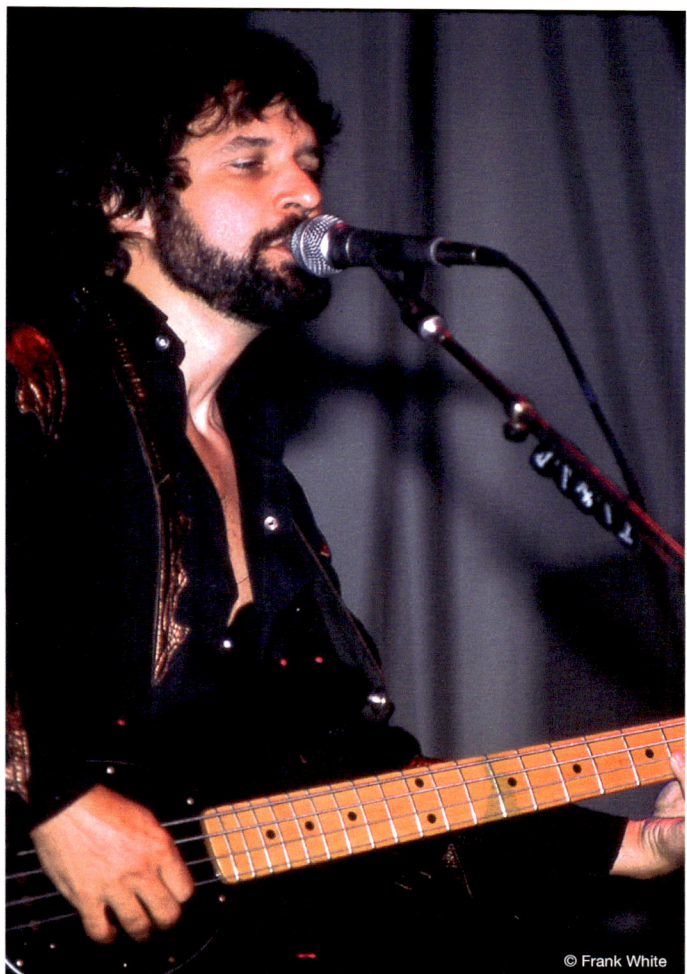

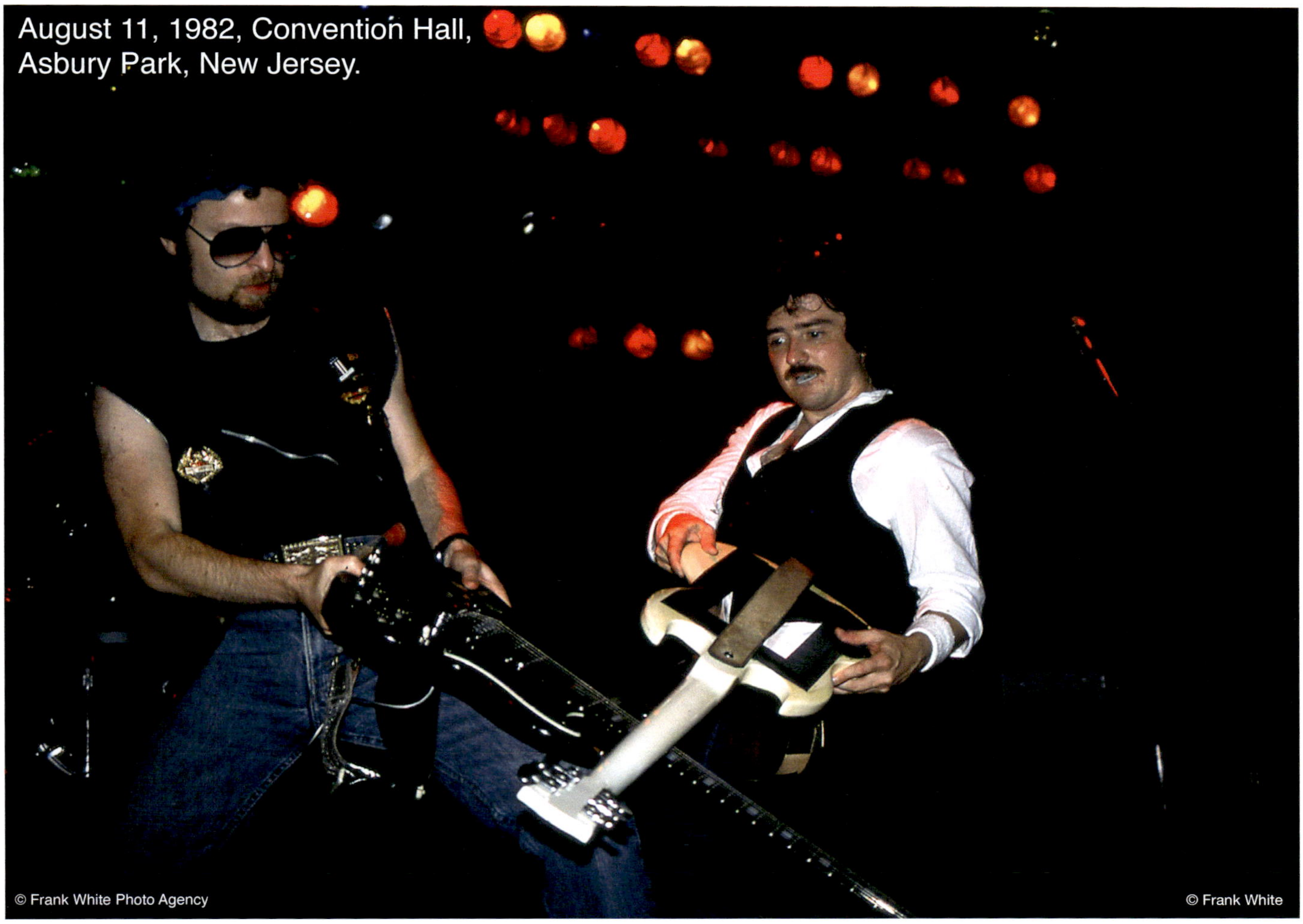

August 11, 1982, Convention Hall, Asbury Park, New Jersey.

© Frank White Photo Agency

© Frank White

February 22, 1984, Capitol Theatre, Passaic, New Jersey.

1983

April – June 1983. The band work at Boogie Hotel in Port Jefferson, NY, Kingdom Sound on Long Island, NY and The Automatt, Studio C, in San Francisco, CA, on tracks slated for their ninth studio album.

November 1, 1983. Columbia issue the ninth Blue Öyster Cult album. *The Revolution by Night*, produced by Loverboy knob-twiddler Bruce Fairbairn. It's the first studio album from the band without Albert Bouchard, who is replaced by Rick Downey, who unwisely is heard hitting a lot of very electronic tom toms. The album reaches #93 on the Billboard 200. The UK result is almost identical at #95. The first single is the album's heavy opening track, "Take Me Away" backed with "Let Go" which is a co-write between Buck, Eric and friend of the band, Ian Hunter of Mott the Hoople fame. In the UK, the B-side is biker tale "Feel the Thunder".

November 16, 1983 – January 17, 1984. The band tour the US promoting *The Revolution by Night*. Main support comes from Aldo Nova, Dokken and Rainbow.

1984

1984. The SETI institute is incorporated. Like BÖC, US scientists are looking for proof of alien life.

1984. Columbia rejects from the band what is essentially an early version of what would emerge in 1988 as *Imaginos*.

1984. Columbia keeps selling "(Don't Fear) The Reaper" issuing it as part of their Back Tracks program, this time with sombre ballad "I Love the Night," from *Spectres*, as the B-side.

January 21 – February 15, 1983. The band conduct an extensive European campaign, supported by Aldo Nova.

February 1984. Columbia go with "Shooting Shark" as a second single from *The Revolution by Night*, backed with "Dragon Lady". The modern pop construct from Donald is topped with a lyric from long-time band friend Patti Smith. The single sees some success, due to its popular MTV video. The single is issued in a picture sleeve in both the US and the UK.

August 4, 1984. The Dream Syndicate issue *Medicine Show*, their second studio album. It is produced by Sandy Pearlman and the keyboard player on the record is Tommy Zvoncheck. A song written by the band's Karl Precoda but not used on the record called "Wings of Mercury" was offered to BÖC, who played it a few times live in 1985 and 1986 as a sort of fast, heavy shuffle. The idea was that the band might include it on their upcoming *Club Ninja* record, but this did not come to pass.

December 22, 1984. After dozens of US tour dates throughout the balance of 1984, Rick Downey plays his last show with the band, at the Agora in New Haven, CT.

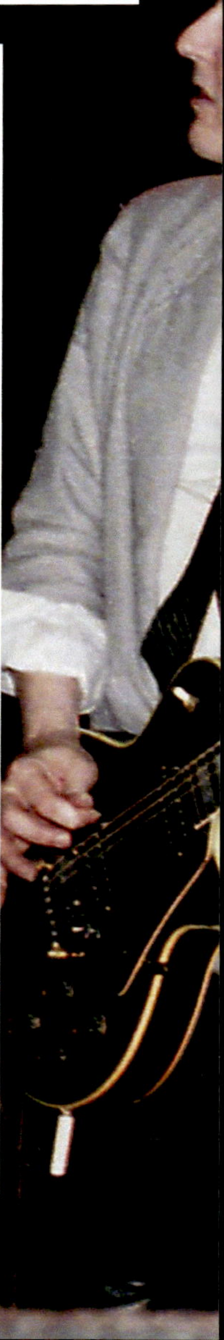

130

February 22, 1984, Capitol Theatre, Passaic, New Jersey.

1985

February 2, 1985. Albert Bouchard rejoins the band, replacing Rick Downey. Bouchard's first show back is at the Civic Auditorium in Redding, CA.

February 11, 1985. Albert's last show of his short second tenure, at Sherwood Hall in Salinas, CA.

April 18, 1985. Jimmy Wilcox joins as the band's new drummer. This is also Tommy Zvoncheck's first show, as replacement for Allen. Most of the US shows in 1985 were billed as Soft White Underbelly dates.

October 17, 1985. The band play a show at The Channel in Boston, at which Eric says, "How 'bout the Red Sox and the Mets in the World Series next year?" Beginning in two days was the 1985 World Series, featuring the Kansas City Royals and the St. Louis Cardinals. A year and a day later, the Boston Red Sox and the New York Mets took the field to begin the best-of-seven finals, with the Mets winning.

November 24 – December 12, 1985. BÖC conduct an extensive UK tour, supported by Girlschool and Statetrooper.

December 10, 1985. Columbia issue the tenth Blue Öyster Cult album, entitled *Club Ninja*. It is disastrously received by the band's dwindling fan base, selling only 175,000 copies, making it the second album in a row from the band not to certify as gold. The band return to Sandy Pearlman for production duties after four albums credited to big-name producers. The first single is "Dancin' in the Ruins" (a rare contribution from "song doctors") backed with "Shadow Warrior" — lyrics from fantasy writer Eric Van Lustbader. The UK goes with "White Flags" backed with "Rock Not War".

1986

1986. Sandy Pearlman gets his own studio. Alpha & Omega begins life in a leased space at Hyde Street Studios but then moves to San Rafael, in Marin County in 1991. Along the way, in 1989, he buys alternative label 415 Records and re-christens it Popular Metaphysics.

January 1, 1986. Ronnie James Dio's heavy metal album for famine relief in Africa, *Hear 'n Aid*, is released. Donald is part of the project, turning in a solo and performing backing vocals.

January 26 – February 23, 1986. The band tours Europe, supported by Tokyo Blade. The February 23rd date at the Metropol in Berlin represents Joe Bouchard's last show with the band.

February 1986. The second and last US single from *Club Ninja* is "Perfect Water" backed with "Spy in the House of Night". The A-side features lyrics from New York poet Jim Carroll and the B-side features lyrics from New York author Richard Meltzer.

March 19, 1986. Jon Rogers joins the band after the departure of founding member Joe Bouchard, who leaves soured by the *Club Ninja* experience. This date takes place at the Civic Auditorium in Santa Cruz, CA, and is supported by Ronnie Montrose.

August 25, 1989, The Bacchanal, San Diego, California.

Photos by Tom Wallace

April 13 – May 2, 1985. The band support Rush on a clutch of US dates. They would follow up this strange career happenstance by supporting Ozzy Osbourne a half dozen times in July.

September 21, 1986. Tommy Zvoncheck leaves the fold and the band goes into a period of inactivity, which lasts through to July '87. This date, with a show in West Virginia, is the last until they play Greece the following summer.

1987

1987. Albert tours with Mamas & the Papas, Peter Noone and the Spencer Davis Group.

1987. Sometime BÖC lyricist David Roter (collaborating with Albert) issues his debut David Roter Band album, *Bambo*. It includes versions of his two BÖC credits "Unknown Tongue" and "Joan Crawford". Roter would issue four albums, each with BÖC connections, before his death from leukemia in 2003 at the age of 56.

Early 1987. After a bewildering army of guest musicians work on *Imaginos*, in waves, mostly in 1984 and 1986, Buck travels to California to record at Sandy's studio, a selection of guitar and vocal parts. Tommy Zvoncheck is there as well, re-recording the keyboard parts.

July 8, 9, 1987. The band, inactive for nearly a year, is reborn when Allen Lanier returns to the fold, and they acquire a new drummer named Ron Riddle. The catalyst comes when Sandy Pearlman and long-suffering manager at this point Steve Schenck land the band these two gigs in Greece, followed by a handful of dates in Switzerland and West Germany.

October 2 – 4, 1987. Eric Bloom and sci-fi literary legend Michael Moorcock perform "Veteran of the Psychic Wars" at the inaugural DragonCon in Atlanta. The duo's first collaboration for Blue Öyster Cult was "The Great Sun Jester" back on *Mirrors*, followed by "Black Blade" on *Cultosaurus Erectus*.

October 23, 1987. John Carpenter's horror flick *Prince of Darkness* hits theatres. A bruise in the form of a BÖC logo appears on the arm of a character called Kelly. Previously, Carpenter had used "(Don't Fear) The Reaper" in his hit slasher film *Halloween*.

1988

February 23 – March 8, 1988. Following an active January and February at home, the band conduct a European tour, primarily of West Germany, supported by Irish rockers Mama's Boys. The balance of the year finds the band with a full dance card of concerts all over America, most notable support coming from King's X (on that band's home turf of Texas) and Circus of Power, aptly, a biker band to appease BÖC's biker following.

Early 1988. Eric records his vocals for *Imaginos*; this constitutes the final recording sessions for the album before moving on to the mix.

Photos by Tom Wallace

July 1988. The long-awaited, oft-discussed *Imaginos* concept album finally sees release, but its sound is uneven, marred by too many cooks in the kitchen. Sandy deemed the album, in print on the back cover, "a bedtime story for the children of the damned". There is no single from the album in the US, but the UK issues a picture sleeve single for the band's remake of fan favourite "Astronomy," backed with "Magna of Illusion". Albert sues the band in a fight to protect his credit as co-producer of the record. He had been estranged from the band, but had done much work on the tracks over the previous six years.

July 13, 1988. The 1978 live album *Some Enchanted Evening* achieves its US platinum certification.

1989

February 1 – April 6, 1989. The band conduct an extensive European campaign, supported by guitarist Patrick Rondat (in his native France), plus Miss Daisy in the UK and Kansas and Steve Morse in West Germany and Switzerland. Otherwise, the band tour pretty much solid all year in the US and Canada.

July 1989. Deadringer issue *Electrocution of the Heart*, on Grudge Records. On keyboards and backing vocals is Joe Bouchard. The album features a version of an unused Blue Öyster Cult number called "Summa Cum Loud". Also in the band are Alice Cooper bassist Dennis Dunaway, with whom Joe would have a long creative association. There's also Ted Nugent vocalist Charlie Huhn and Alice Cooper drummer Neal Smith, co-writer of "Shadow of California" on *The Revolution by Night*.

"I would say BÖC is somewhere between our heyday and the Rock and Roll Hall of Fame. But the fact is, is that we haven't put out any important recorded work for awhile. Probably at the bottom of that has been a lack of will to really do anything stupendous, as far as new material. Now that's not to say that it won't happen, because we've got a lot of good stuff that's boiling under right now. We'd like to make another record that really means something, and I think we're working towards that. But to be frank, after doing it for 15 years, and the band being together for 20, there wasn't really a lot left to say. So rather than just churn out mediocre stuff, why not just not do anything? It hasn't hurt us, to not to go ahead and not put out a bad record. So I guess the plan is to get something stunning before we do it again."

Donald "Buck Dharma" Roeser

The 1990s

The 1990s marked a decade of frustration for the fans, who were constantly speculating when a new record would arrive, exacerbated by the fact that the band were still active and touring and occasionally teasing out talk of new product. Also tempting the taste buds were new songs along the way on weird and unsatisfying records like the *Bad Channels* soundtrack ("Demon's Kiss" and "The Horsemen Arrive") and the *Summerdaze* compilation ("Power Underneath Despair").

On the sidelines, Joe was contemplating his next move and Albert was starting to get productive. Meanwhile BÖC kept up the theme of issuing weird records like *Cult Classic* featuring re-recordings of their hits but also the first serious compilation in *Workshop of the Telescopes*, which served to keep interest on the boil.

But then there it was, in 1998, an all-new record, excepting an intimate, acoustic re-do of "In Thee". *Heaven Forbid* found the band moving forward, working upon a hard surface built of modern technology, Buck and Eric riffing, chugging, paying attention to details along the way. Highlights included Eric's "See You in Black," one of the band's heaviest rockers ever, but also two light and lush Donald numbers in "Live for Me" and "Harvest Moon".

It's unfortunate the album cover was a bit of a botch, because the music enclosed proved that the band cared and were not willing to phone it in. In any event, by the end of the decade all was forgiven as the band not only delivered an album but kept touring hard despite spending the last fifteen years knocked down a few pegs.

February 7, 1991, Park Place, El Cajon, California.

Photo by Tom Wallace

Photo by Tom Wallace

142

1990

1990. CBS Special Products issue a BÖC compilation called *On Flame with Rock and Roll*.

February 1 – December 15, 1990. Well into their daily lives as a "working band," the members of BÖC play runs of dates all over America, totalling between fifty and sixty, visiting clubs, theatres and acquainting themselves with the country fair circuit.

March 10 – June 16, 1990. The Red and the Black — Buck Dharma, Jon Rogers and Ron Riddle — tour local to New York as The Red and the Black.

April 1990. Columbia issues a compilation called *Career of Evil*.

1991

1991. Castle issue a semi-official BÖC live album called *Live 1976*.

January 18 – December 15, 1991. The band's touring schedule is very much similar to that of the previous year, dates all around America with a variety of support acts, and no trips overseas. On February 12th at the Crest Theatre in Sacramento, CA, Steve Morse comes on and plays "Roadhouse Blues" with the band. In May, for a stretch, the band is supported by Hall Aflame, an excellent roots metal project commandeered by Metal Church's Kurdt Vanderhoof.

June 6, 1991. Ron Riddle leaves the band, to be replaced by Chuck Bürgi, who plays his first show on this date, in Grand Rapids, MI.

1992

May 11, 1992. *Secret Treaties* is certified gold in the US, for sales of over 500,000 copies.

May 15, 1992. John Miceli joins the band, playing his first show on this date at Sneakers in San Antonio, Texas.

May 24, 1992. The band plays a show in Maryland Heights, Missouri on a flatbed truck in a parking lot.

June 17, 1993. Chuck Bürgi returns, replacing John Miceli and playing his first gig on this date in Louisville, Kentucky.

June 25, 1992. Sci-fi spoof *Bad Channels* is issued. BÖC are a big part of the soundtrack album.

August 4, 1992. Moonstone Records issues the *Bad Channels* soundtrack album. Included are a bunch of songs by no-name bands but also an original score by BÖC, which is typical soundtrack music, but with lots of Buck licks. It's a bit like instrumental Pink Floyd from the eighties. There are also two new songs, "Demon's Kiss" and "The Horsemen Arrive" — the first an energetic hard rocker with hot Buck soloing and the second a slow epic heavy metal monster.

September 24 – October 13, 1993. The band conduct a European tour, with most of the dates taking place in Germany.

Photo by Tom Wallace

1993

1993. Europe sees the release of a 16-track compilation called *Best – The Reaper*.

November 5 – December 4, 1993. Another typical year of dates all over America gets interesting by this point, where the band join forces with Nazareth, Uriah Heep and Wishbone Ash for a massive classic rock package which splits dates between the US and Canada.

December 8 – December 20, 1993. The novel classic rock package concept from the previous few weeks is perpetuated overseas, where BÖC play with Molly Hatchet, Uriah Heep and Girlschool all over Germany, with the closing date taking place in Vienna, Austria.

1994

February 18 – December 31, 1994. BÖC continue to pack their lunchboxes and hit the road despite not issuing any new product in six years, playing approximately ninety dates across America, a few a month, every month except March.

June 1994. Caroline and SPV issue *Cult Classic*, on which the band re-record their hits. The dubious album also sees release by other labels as *Champions of Rock* and *E.T.I. Revisited*. The lineup for the record features original members Eric, Buck and Allen, along with Chuck Bürgi and Jon Rogers.

October 18, 1994. The Brain Surgeons, Albert's band with his wife Deb Frost, issue their first album, entitled *Eponymous*.

1995

1995. Rick Downey returns to the BÖC fold, tour managing a string of dates.

May 27, 1995. Greg Smith replaces Jon Rogers, but is out of the band by September, moving on to Ritchie Blackmore's Rainbow. Rogers' last show is in Toronto on April 8th, with Greg tuning up his bass for a show on this date at Pine Knobs in Detroit, BÖC playing alongside April Wine. Into June, Greg will find himself playing with the band at a Harley Davidson party and a hot air balloon festival out at an airport in Atlanta.

August 11, 1995. Danny Miranda replaces Greg Smith on bass.

August 21, 1995. Ritchie Blackmore's Rainbow issue a studio album of new material called *Stranger in Us All*. BOC alumni Greg Smith and John O. Reilly are bassist and drummer on the project respectively.

John Micelli, better known for his time with Meat Loaf, deputised for Chuck Bürgi during a tour in the summer of 1992.

Bassist and backing vocalist Greg Smith toured briefly with the Cult in the summer of 1995.

Former Brand X and Rainbow drummer Chuck Bürgi was the pounding rhythm during most of the nineties.

September 15, 1995. Drummer Chuck Bürgi leaves the band, replaced by John O. Reilly, most recently of Ritchie Blackmore's Rainbow. Now Chuck, along with Greg Smith, joins Rainbow. Reilly plays his first gig with the band on this date in Waterloo, Iowa, followed the next night by a motorcycle rally at the Cherokee Ceremonial Grounds in North Carolina.

September 26, 1995. Columbia issues a professional, well-appointed two-CD compilation called *Workshop of the Telescopes*, featuring all the hits and a handful of minor rarities.

Late 1995. Albert's The Brain Surgeons issue their second album, *Trepanation*. Brother Joe guests on three tracks, providing vocals and mandolin.

December 13 – 16, 1995. The band close out a moderately active year of US and Canadian dates with four shows in Europe, playing London, Paris and Greece.

1996

1996. The Brian Surgeons issue their third album, *Box of Hammers*. Joe Bouchard returns as guest, providing keyboards.

April 1996. The Internet is brand-new and Eric Bloom is an early adopter, using AOL and playing Gemstone III, a pioneering role-playing game. He also conducts BÖC online live chats and is active on the band's message board.

August 1996. Drummer John O. Reilly leaves the band, returning to tour dates with Ritchie Blackmore's Rainbow. He is replaced by a returning Chuck Bürgi as the band fill the year with US dates and the occasional foray north of the border.

1997

1997. The Brain Surgeons issue odds and sods album *Malpractise*, which includes version of a number of BÖC songs.

February 21, 1997. Drummer Bobby Rondinelli joins the band. Much of the band's long-awaited forthcoming studio album is already recorded, with Chuck Bürgi on drums. Bobby's first gig with the band is on this date in Pittsfield, Massachusetts.

April 11, 1997. Donald, his wife Sandy plus BÖC members John Micelli and Danny Miranda perform a benefit concert in Atlanta, GA in support of ten-year-old Ricky Browning, who sadly succumbs to his diagnosis of a brain tumour. Buck and Sandy keep close relations with the family after Ricky's death.

May 30 – July 4, 1997. The band embarks on the Summerdaze festival package, which generates a CD commemorating the tour. Helping BÖC conjure nostalgic thoughts are Steppenwolf, Foghat and Pat Travers. Ronnie Montrose joins the band on stage for "(Don't Fear) The Reaper" at the Universal Amphitheatre on June 27th. The *Summerdaze* album, issued by CMC, included three tracks from BÖC, live versions of "(Don't Fear) The Reaper" and "Godzilla" along with a studio rendition of a triumphant new heavy metal rocker called "Power Underneath Despair".

August 9, 10, 1997. Highlight of a typical touring year for the band includes this trip to Denmark to play with Status Quo and the Mick Taylor's Blues Band.

1998

1998. Sony in Germany issue a 14-track BÖC compilation called *Tattoo Vampire*. Meanwhile in the US and Australia, there's a compilation called *Super Hits*.

March 24, 1998. Now on the CMC label, BÖC issue their first new studio album in ten years, entitled *Heaven Forbid*. Recorded over time, there are two bassists who play on the album, Danny Miranda and Jon Rogers, plus two drummers, Chuck Bürgi and Bobby Rondinelli, although Rondinelli plays on only one track, "Live for Me". Science fiction writer John Shirley pens many of the album's lyrics. The band tour heavily throughout '98 in support of the new record.

May 20, 1998. A big budget blockbuster remake of *Godzilla* hits theatres. Offended that they weren't asked to be involved, the band release "Nozilla," a remake of "Godzilla" with all-new lyrics that complain lightheartedly about the situation. The track is released exclusively to radio stations.

November 24, 1998. In what is probably the most prominent (and lucrative) cover of a Blue Öyster Cult song, Metallica include a rendition of "Astronomy" on their two-CD covers album *Garage Inc.* The Metallica guys have also said that the title of their song "Harvester of Sorrow" was inspired by "Harvester of Eyes". As well, Lars Ulrich has done multiple interviews wearing a Blue Öyster Cult shirt.

1999

1999. The Brain Surgeons issue a double album called *Piece of Work*. Meanwhile this year also yields *Too Hip for the Room – Don't Fear the Remake: Selections from the Blue Öyster Cult Songbook*. The odds 'n' songs comedic record includes cameos from Danny Miranda, John Shirley, Buck, Eric, and expert on all things Cult, Bolle Gregmar.

January 29 – March 4, 1999. Al Pitrelli steps in for an ailing Allen Lanier, before moving on to Megadeth.

March 17, 1999. Allen Lanier's first gig back is on a chilly night in Albuquerque, New Mexico, playing in a tent in a parking lot.

May 8 – May 23, 1999. Another year packed with North American dates is highlighted by concerts in Hawaii, Guam and Japan, where the band often do two shows a day. Back home it's the usual assortment of ribfests, state fairs, biker gatherings, clubs and casinos.

November 2, 1999. Sebastian Bach's live album *Bring 'Em Bach Alive!* includes a cover of "Godzilla".

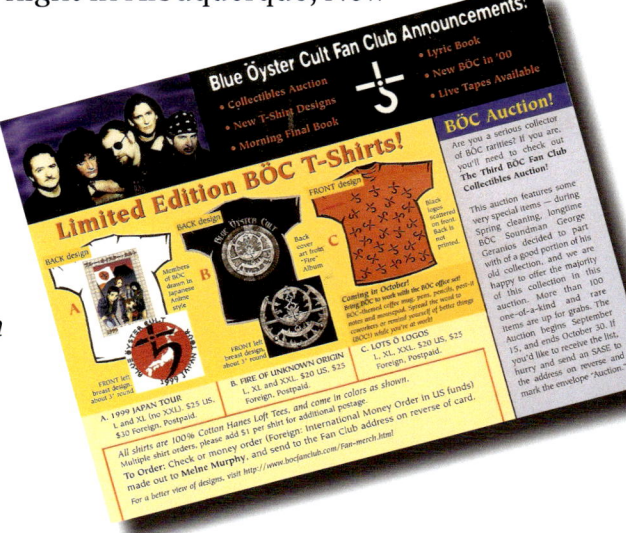

"John Shirley is very prolific and always very much rooted in his novel writing. He's very entertaining in his way. He writes tons of lyrics and sends them to Eric and I. Eric and I tend to like different styles of John's lyrics. I look for the ones that suit my sensibility and Eric goes for the ones that suit his. I've written lyrics but I'm terribly self-critical and take a long time. I'm very shy about exposing my words. I would rather use someone else's words but they have to resonate with me for me to do it. I'm very happy to work with John. John was actually introduced to us by Sandy. William Gibson actually credits John with the whole cyberspace thing. He actually created it and William Gibson kind of cadged it from him."

Donald "Buck Dharma" Roeser

The 2000s Through 2020

It's understandable that all our favourite heritage bands either retire or begin to cut back the schedule, but Blue Öyster Cult's long stretch between albums since 1988 has been particularly disconcerting for the fans. We appreciate that Buck and Eric, now nearing their 80s, continue to tour and tour regularly, really, basically all the time but with enough days off so that they don't drop dead.

As we edged into the 2000s, fortunately *Curse of the Hidden Mirror* was a fine record, intriguingly not heavy but then sophisticated and singular of sound. It's fresh and different for BÖC, but sensibly somewhat linked to the style of the mid-heavy songs from *Heaven Forbid*. But after that, we settled into this long concert-only relationship with the guys, the nice part being that new life has been breathed into the band by Danny Miranda, Jules Radino and Richie Castellano, who shine across increasingly adventurous set lists regularly studded with songs that delight the old guard.

Then in 2020 we got a new album, *The Symbol Remains*, long, quite heavy, varied and ultimately effusively received. All was right again between band and fan, and any previous absences had been excused and forgotten. Then came more live gigs, more live releases, and arguably the band's career has been more action-packed post-pandemic than it's been for years.

Another fortunate development is that, at first, Albert and Deb Frost as Brain Surgeons, and then Joe and Albert as part of Blue Coupe and Joe as a solo act, proved to be crazy productive over the last 24 years, extending a brand that previously had coughed up a single solo project in Buck's *Flat Out* album of 1982. In conjunction, relations between Buck and Eric and the Bouchards had thawed enough to allow various forms of reunion.

In the end, there is one goal left that would be nice to see achieved for the boys: let's get Blue Öyster Cult into the Rock and Roll Hall of Fame. With a level head, I might not have thought it reasonable to expect ten or 15 years ago, but seeing the crop yields in recent years, yeah, BÖC's accomplishments are more than on par.

Tour Poster from 2002

2000

January 17, 2000. Helen Wheels dies, at the age of 50, in Ithaca, NY after contracting an infection following recent corrective surgery on her back (in later life, Helen had become a body builder).

February 8, 2000. Legacy/Columbia issue *Don't Fear the Reaper: The Best of Blue Öyster Cult*.

April 8, 2000. The "More Cowbell" sketch airs, on Saturday Night Live. Starring Will Ferrell and Christopher Walken, the sketch presents a loosely fictionalized version of BÖC recording "(Don't Fear) The Reaper" with Walken immortalized forever after as the producer imploring that the song needs more cowbell. Various weird and easily verifiable factual errors, plus deliberate inaccuracies, lend the clip additional mystery and mystique. Actual co-producer on the album David Lucas (and not either of the Bruce Dickinsons in the music business! — in the sketch, "*the* Bruce Dickinson" is the producer) has said that he, in fact, was the one who played cowbell on the 1976 recording of the song, and not the fictional Gene Frenkle, played by Ferrell.

December 11, 2000 – March 2001. The band work at Millbrook Studios in Millbrook, NY on the recordings that will comprise their fourteenth studio album.

2001

April 23, 2001. Elektra/Rhino issue *St. Cecilia: The Elektra Recordings*, comprising more than an album's worth of unreleased material from the band recorded in 1970 when they were called Stalk-Forrest Group.

June 5, 2001. Blue Öyster Cult issue a fourteenth studio album, entitled *Curse of the Hidden Mirror*. The title of the record is the name of an old Stalk-Forrest Group song. John Shirley returns as the band's primary lyricist. Recording lineup for the album consists of original members Donald, Eric and Allen, plus bassist Danny Miranda and drummer Bobby Rondinelli.

June 21, 2001. Albert's and Deb's record label Cellsum Records issue *To Helen with Love!*, credited to Brain Surgeons and Friends. Numerous members of the extended BÖC family are involved in this loving tribute to the departed Helen Wheels.

June 26, 2001. Columbia issue a promo CD called *God Save Blue Öyster Cult from Themselves: Blue Öyster Cult Expanded Editions Sampler* in conjunction with the ensuing expanded remasters program. Initially released are deluxe editions of the first four studio albums. There are two tracks only available on the sampler, a live version of "Hot Rails to Hell" and Soft White Underbelly demo "John L. Sullivan".

2002

2002. Donald and his wife post to the web, The Dharmas, a comical look at the couple's family life.

May 14 – May 20, 2002. The band tours the UK for the first time in four years, with the last date, in Glasgow, taking place on a ferry boat.

June 21, 2002. The band plays the show that will be documented on live album, *A Long Day's Night*. It takes place at the Navy Pier's Skyline Stage in Chicago.

September 24, 2002. Sanctuary issue a BÖC live album called *A Long Day's Night*. The title of the album derives from the fact that the concert documented took place on the summer solstice, the longest day of the year. Featuring the expected hits but also a handful of obscurities like "Dance on Stilts", "Perfect Water" and "Mistress of the Salmon Salt (Quicklime Girl)". The fine set was also issued on a companion DVD, which is six selections longer than the strictly audio release. Personnel on the project consists of Eric, Buck and Allen with Danny Miranda and Bobby Rondinelli.

2003

2003. Sony Music Custom Marketing Group issue a ten-track compilation called *Are You Ready to Rock?*

February 16, 2003. Long-time friend and BÖC collaborator David Roter loses his battle with cancer. The band dedicates "(Don't Fear) The Reaper" and the encore to Roter at a gig in Yucaipa, California.

March 18, 2003. CMC International issue a compilation called *Then and Now*.

April 1, 2003. Sony issues a compilation called *The Essential Blue Öyster Cult*.

June 2 – 12, 2003. Amidst a lighter than average year of North American dates, the band mount a substantial UK campaign.

June 21, 2003. The Brain Surgeons issue *Beach Party*.

October 25, 2003. At a show in Tampa Bay, Florida, Eric is sick so Buck steps up and does vocals on every song.

December 2003. Richie Castellano is the band's live engineer; he would soon work up the ranks to full band member.

December 3 – December 19, 2003. BÖC support Uriah Heep in that band's best territory, Germany. Third on the bill is Fireball Ministry.

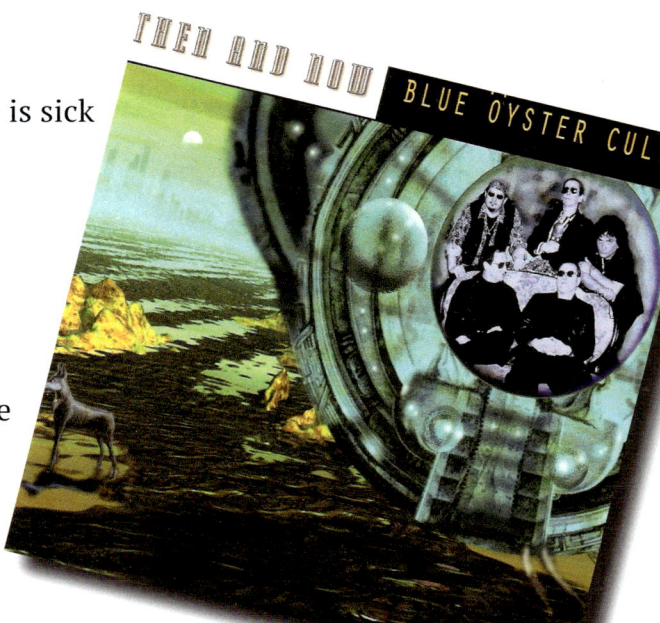

© Alan Perry Concert Photography

June 8, 2003,
The Robin 2, Bilston, UK.

June 8, 2003,
The Robin 2, Bilston, UK.
Pictured is Danny Miranda.

Bobby Rondinelli, drummer for the band from 1997 to 2004.

January 23, 2004,
BB King's Jazz Club, New York.

2004

September 18, 2004. Richie Castellano performs first gig as band bassist, in Las Vegas, Nevada. He replaces Danny Miranda. Also at this time, drummer Bobby Rondinelli leaves the band, to be replaced by Jules Radino.

January 23, 2004, BB King's Jazz Club, New York.

© Alan Perry Concert Photography

June 15, 2004,
The Robin 2, Bilston, UK.

June 15, 2004,
The Robin 2, Bilston, UK.

© Alan Perry Concert Photography

© Alan Perry Concert Photography

June 15, 2004,
The Robin 2, Bilston, UK

January 28, 2005,
BB King's Jazz Club, New York.

2005

March 19, 2005. Queen + Paul Rodgers play their first show ever, in South Africa. Bassist in the band at this one-off Nelson Mandela 46664 Aids Awareness benefit is Danny Miranda, who would subsequently become the band's touring bassist when regular dates begin back in the UK.

June 23, 2005. Sandy Pearlman gives a talk called "Fast, Cheap and Out of Control" at the Purcell Rooms in London's South Bank Centre. The occasion was Patti Smith's Meltdown Festival.

August 30, 2005. At a show in Monroe, Washington, Buck is under the weather, so Eric and Richie do all the singing. Otherwise it's a typical year for these working men, a moderately busy dance card playing in North America only, very much like 2004.

Percussive maestro for the band since 2004, Jules Radino.

© Alan Perry Concert Photography

January 28, 2005,
BB King's Jazz Club, New York.

January 28, 2005,
BB King's Jazz Club, New York.

January 28, 2005,
BB King's Jazz Club, New York.

© Alan Perry Concert Photography

January 28, 2005,
BB King's Jazz Club, New York.
Pictured: Richie Castellano, multi-instrumentalist.

January 27, 2006,
BB King's Jazz Club, New York.
The legendary Allen Lanier, in his last year as part of the band and seven years before his death.

© Alan Perry Concert Photography

2006

2006. Eric Bloom collaborates with artist Phillippe Renaudin on six custom-painted guitars, with each to be played live before being sold.

March 7, 2006. The Brain Surgeons, as Brain Surgeons NYC, issue *Denial of Death*.

September 2006. Allen Lanier leaves the band, never to return, amidst a fairly heavy year of dates for the band, over eighty shows, approximately ten more than 2004 and twenty more than 2005.

January 27, 2006,
BB King's Jazz Club, New York.

This was the second of two concerts. Ex-BOC drummer Albert Bouchard was in the audience.

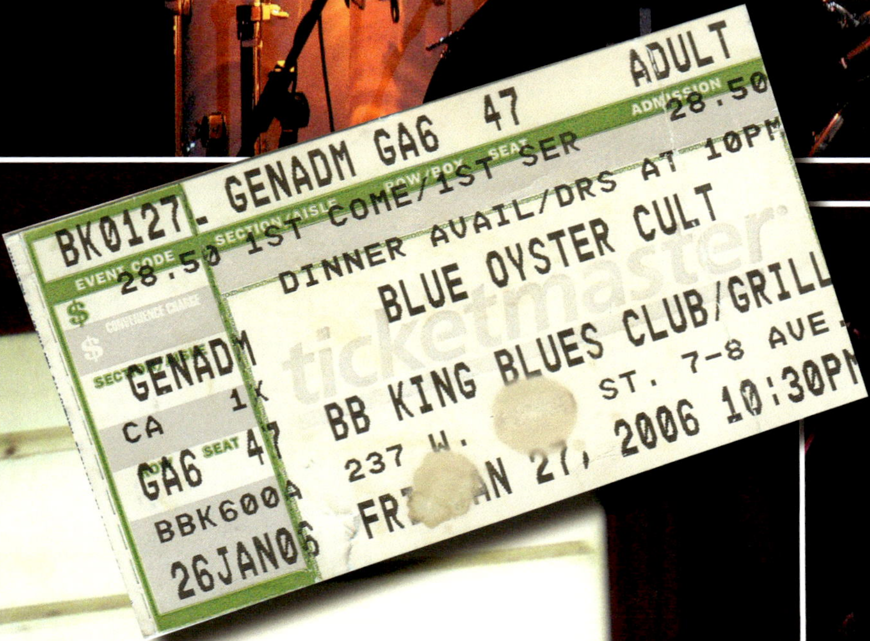

© Alan Perry Concert Photography

183

January 27, 2006,
BB King's Jazz Club, New York.

© Alan Perry Concert Photography

January 27, 2006,
BB King's Jazz Club, New York.

187

January 27, 2006,
BB King's Jazz Club, New York.

© Alan Perry Concert Photography

January 27, 2006,
BB King's Jazz Club, New York.

The Brain Surgeons
January 28, 2006,
Delancey's Bar, New York.

© Alan Perry Concert Photography

The Brain Surgeons
January 28, 2006,
Delancey's Bar, New York.

© Alan Perry Concert Photography

January 26, 2007,
BB King's Jazz Club, New York.

© Alan Perry Concert Photography

2007

February 22, 2007. Joe Bouchard puts out an instructional DVD called *Rock Bass for Beginners*.

Early 2007. Allen Lanier retires. Also at this time, Danny Miranda returns to the band on bass, with Richie Castellano moving over to rhythm guitar and keyboards.

June 2007. Quiet Riot, Ozzy Osbourne and Whitesnake great Rudy Sarzo joins the band on bass, after a brief period when Jon Rogers sits in as band bassist as replacement for Danny Miranda.

October 11, 2007. The Allen Telescope Array becomes operational, at Hat Creek Radio Observatory, 290 miles northeast of San Francisco.

November 3, 2007. The band play a date in Trinidad along with Kansas and local acts. This caps off a robust year of dates studded with ribfests and biker parties.

December 2007. *Imaginos* sees its only CD reissue, through Sony imprint Beat Records. The remaster fixes some of the problems concerning volume levels found on the original 1988 issue.

January 26, 2007,
BB King's Jazz Club, New York.

January 26, 2007,
BB King's Jazz Club, New York.

© Alan Perry Concert Photography

January 2007, BB King's Jazz Club, New York.

Richie moved from bass to guitar and keyboards to replace Allen Lanier, who was absent for medical reasons. Danny Miranda was back on bass after a stint with Queen.

Set-list:
Stairway to the Stars
OD'd on Life
Burning for You
Shooting Shark
Golden Age of Leather
She's as Beautiful as a Foot
Cities on Flame
I Love the Night
Godzilla
(Don't Fear) The Reaper
The Red and the Black

January 26, 2007,
BB King's Jazz Club, New York.

January 27, 2007,
BB King's Jazz Club, New York.

Set-list:
Stairway to the Stars
Burning for You
I Love the Night
Shooting Shark
Buck's Boogie
She's as Beautiful as a Foot
Cities on Flame
Godzilla
Buck Solo
(Don't Fear) The Reaper
Astronomy

© Alan Perry Concert Photography

January 27, 2007,
BB King's Jazz Club, New York.

© Alan Perry Concert Photography

208

January 27, 2007,
BB King's Jazz Club, New York.

© Alan Perry Concert Photography

June 9, 2008, The Robin 2, Bilston, UK.

© Alan Perry Concert Photography

2008

2008. Albert and Joe, with Alice Cooper bassist Dennis Dunaway, form Blue Coupe.

2008. Tommy Zvoncheck issues his first solo album. *ZKG* features a guest slot by Donald on a track called "Storm Chaser".

June 4 – June 15, 2008. The band play a handful of mainland European dates followed by a substantial English campaign, this in the middle of a very busy year of over 100 shows with personnel movements involving Rudy Sarzo, Danny Miranda, Bobby Rondinelli, Richie Castellano and Tommy Zvoncheck.

June 9, 2008, The Robin 2, Bilston, UK.

Set list:
(as abbreviated for the band members)
Summer
34
Career
Burning
Bux Boogie
Harvest Moon
Vigil
ME262
Joan
Golden Age
Last Days/Vets/Astro
Godzilla
Reaper

© Alan Perry Concert Photography

June 9, 2008, The Robin 2, Bilston, UK.

© Alan Perry Concert Photography

June 9, 2008, The Robin 2, Bilston, UK.

© Alan Perry Concert Photography

2009

2009. Sandy is named a member-at-large for the Library of Congress' National Recording Preservation Board.

December 12, 13, 2009. Two shows in Greece cap off a below average touring year for the band of under 60 dates.

2010

August 7, 2010. Arguable highlight of a 75-date year for the band comes on this night when BÖC support Aerosmith at a shed show in Tampa, Florida. Putting the damper on the night however was the fact that the sound was atrocious, the band was not broadcast on the screens, and the set consisted of a mere six songs spanning forty-nine minutes.

November 9, 2010. Blue Coupe issue *Tornado on the Tracks*.

June 9, 2008, The Robin 2, Bilston, UK.

© Alan Perry Concert Photography

September 2, 2012, Last Fling Fest, Rotary Park, Napierville, Illinois.

Photo by Greg Olma

2011

June 29, 2011. Engineer on many key projects David Lucas is inducted into the Buffalo Music Hall of Fame.

July 2, 2011. Buck joins Cheap Trick on stage at the Greely Stampede in Greely, Clorodao for the band's performance of "Ain't That a Shame". This is amidst a typical year of about seventy shows, similar to the schedule in 2010.

Late 2011. Richie Castellano scores a viral video hit with his all-hands-on-deck version of "Bohemian Rhapsody."

September 2, 2012, Last Fling Fest, Rotary Park, Napierville, Illinois.

September 2, 2012, Last Fling Fest, Rotary Park, Napierville, Illinois.

Photos by Greg Olma

September 2, 2012, Last Fling Fest, Rotary Park, Napierville, Illinois.

Photo by Greg Olma

Photo by Greg Olma

September 2, 2012, Last Fling Fest, Rotary Park, Napierville, Illinois.

Photos by Greg Olma

September 2, 2012, Last Fling Fest, Rotary Park, Napierville, Illinois.

Photo by Greg Olma

Photo by Greg Olma

2012

January 27, 2012. At the annual NAMM music industry convention in LA, BÖC perform a three-song acoustic set.

June 8 – June 17, 2012. The band spice up their year with another short European tour, including a show at Hellfest in France.

July 1, 2012. The band announce that Kasim Sulton of Utopia fame has joined the band, on bass and vocals. This follows the departure of Rudy Sarzo to Animetal USA. Kasim would be on board for five years.

August 21, 2012. Joe Bouchard issues a solo album called *Tales from the Island*.

October 27, 2012. The band performs their first ever acoustic show, at the Jeanne Rimsky Theater in Port Washington, NY.

October 30, 2012. A massive reissue project by Sony/Legacy results in *The Columbia Albums Collection* box set. The package includes 16 CDs and is stuffed with rarities and radio performances.

November 5, 2012. Allen Lanier joins the band one last time for a fortieth anniversary concert at the Best Buy Theater in New York City featuring all five original members. The date had been rescheduled from October 28th, due to the approach of Hurricane Sandy.

2013

January 10 – 12, 2013. The band play the Rock Legends Cruise.

April 18 – 25, 2013. The band tour Australia for the first time ever, anchored by two performances at the Dig It Up! Festival put on by local alt-rock heroes Hoodoo Gurus.

April 30, 2013. Blue Coupe issue a sophomore album of original material called *Million More Miles*.

August 14, 2013. Allen Lanier dies, succumbing to complications from COPD. He was survived at the time by his wife Dory, sister Mary Anne and mother Martha.

2014

July 29, 2014. Albert Bouchard issues a solo album called *Incantation*, which includes novel interpretations of "Death Valley Nights" and "Career of Evil."

October 11, 2014. The guys "land" another cruise gig, this time sailing from Stockholm to Helsinki.

September 30, 2016, Rock Carnival, First Energy Park, Lakewood, New Jersey.

October 17, 2014. The band plays a date at the Hard Rock in Northfield, Ohio which will be immortalized on a live album six years later.

December 12, 2014. Joe Bouchard issues a solo album called *Jukebox in My Head*.

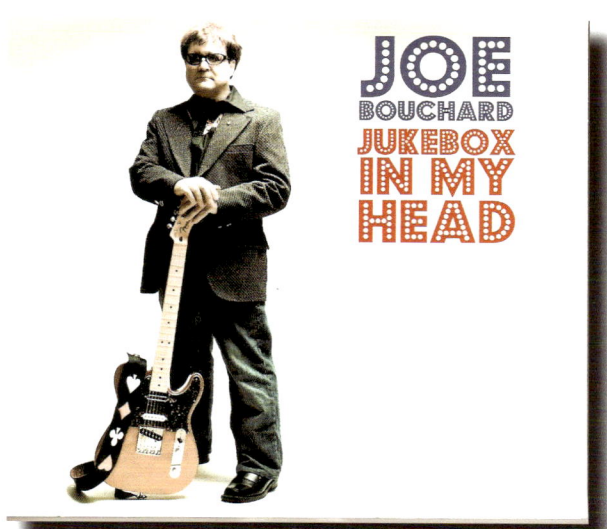

2015

January 1, 2015. Donald issues on Soundcloud, a new solo song called "Fight".

February 19 – 21, 2015. The band partake of another cruise gig, travelling from Ft. Lauderdale to the Bahamas.

February 24, 2015. At a show in West Palm Beach, Florida, David Lucas guests on cowbell.

March 20, 2015. At a New York date, Albert guests for the encore.

August 13, 2015. Buck signs on to endorse Kiesel Carvin Guitars, having previously been a fan of the company's Vader V6.

October 20, 2015. J.K. Rowling, under her alias Robert Galbraith, sees publication of her crime novel *Career of Evil*, in which a character receives a message quoting from BÖC song, "Mistress of the Salmon Salt (Quicklime Girl)".

December 2015. Sandy Pearlman suffers a cerebral haemorrhage.

2016

2016. *Secret Treaties* is issued in Super Audio CD format.

June 17, 2016. A BÖC gig at BB King's in New York City includes very special guests Albert and Joe Bouchard, who perform a show designated a tribute to Allen Lanier.

July 26, 2016. Sandy Pearlman dies, aged 72, Marin County, California, not far from the Cliff House featured on the cover of *Imaginos*. Cause of death was pneumonia due to stroke-related complications.

July 28, 2016. The band plays in Ireland (Dublin) for the first time ever. There is also a London show the following night. Albert Bouchard guests on these special shows, which also feature *Agents of Fortune* performed in its entirety, to celebrate its fortieth anniversary — granted, this follows upon similar events in the US. Otherwise, 2016 is another standard year of approximately seventy-five dates.

2017

Early 2017. Danny Miranda returns to the fold on bass, replacing Kasim Sulton. This solidifies the BÖC lineup as it exists to this day: Donald Roeser, Eric Bloom, Richie Castellano, Danny Miranda and Jules Radino.

June 16 – July 1, 2017. The band enjoy festival season in Europe, while also mounting a mini-tour with Queensrÿche. All told, the year yields over ninety dates for the band.

September 25, 2017. Joe Bouchard issues a solo album called *Playin' History*.

2018

February 15 – 18, 2018. The band enjoy another cruise ship gig, to kick of a year of nearly eighty US and Canadian dates.

November 23, 2018. *Some Enchanted Evening* is re-released on vinyl for Record Store Day. This is a "Legacy Edition" double vinyl with seven bonus tracks and is pressed on blue translucent vinyl. It is configured as a gatefold and limited to 3,000 copies. This follows upon a tradition of rarities vinyl records issued on previous Record Store Days.

2019

February 21 – March 1, 2019. The band tour England, supported by The Temperance Movement. It's all part of an impressive dance card of approximately eighty dates in a year when Donald "Buck Dharma" Roeser turns 72 and Eric "Manny" Bloom turns 75.

July 10, 2019. Blue Öyster Cult sign with Italy-based Frontiers Music, for a new studio album plus an extensive reissue program.

November 11, 2019. Blue Coupe issue *Eleven Even*.

2020

January 24, 2020. The band sees the simultaneous release of two albums, a reissue of *Cult Classic* and a live set (available on DVD, blu-Ray, triple vinyl and double CD) called *Hard Rock Live Cleveland 2014*.

March 6, 2020. Frontiers issue *Agents of Fortune 40th Anniversary Live 2016* as well as a new edition of the band's 1998 studio album, *Heaven Forbid*. Anticipation mounts for the long awaited new Blue Öyster Cult studio album now in progress...

April 2020. Working at Mercy College Studio A in Dobbs Ferry, New York, the band complete work on their long-awaited new studio album.

February 27, 2019,
The O2 Institute, Birmingham.

© Alan Perry Concert Photography

February 27, 2019,
The O2 Institute, Birmingham.

Set list:
(as abbreviated for the band members)
Red Black
B4 Kiss
Summer of Love
Burnin
Perfect Water
Harvest or Shark
Vigil
ETI
Bux Boogie
Last Days
Ruins
Godzilla
Reaper

© Alan Perry Concert Photography

August 7, 2020. Frontiers issues a third BÖC live album in quick succession, called *45th Anniversary – Live in London*.

August 28, 2020. Having earlier in the month revealed the artwork and full track listing of their new album, Blue Öyster Cult issue on streaming services two new songs, "That Was Me" and "Box in My Head."

September 1, 2020. Frontiers Music issue a video for "That Was Me." The band invite back exiled drummer Albert Bouchard, co-architect of *Imaginos* with Sandy Pearlman, to bang on a cowbell.

September 10, 2020. "Box in My Head," also gets video treatment, followed two weeks later with a third track, "Tainted Blood," seeing audio and video release.

October 9, 2020. Blue Öyster Cult issue their first album in 19 years, entitled *The Symbol Remains*. Weighing in at 14 tracks and just over an hour, the album is produced by Buck, Eric and Richie. On this day, a video clip for "The Alchemist" appears on YouTube, making it the fourth video from the album. Japan gets an acoustic version of opener "That Was Me" as a bonus track. The album nips onto the lower rungs of the official Billboard 200 chart, achieving a No.192 placement.

November 26, 2020. Albert Bouchard issues a solo album called *Re Imaginos*. He calls it a correction, meaning a correction upon the 1988 *Imaginos* album. The songs have been re-sequenced, and the musical arrangements pared back, in accordance with Sandy's original late '60s vision for the *Imaginos* album.

2021

January 10, 2021. Blue Öyster Cult cover artist Greg Scott dies, due to complications from a heart attack.

October 22, 2021. Albert Bouchard issues *Imaginos II: Bombs Over Germany (Minus Zero and Counting)*.

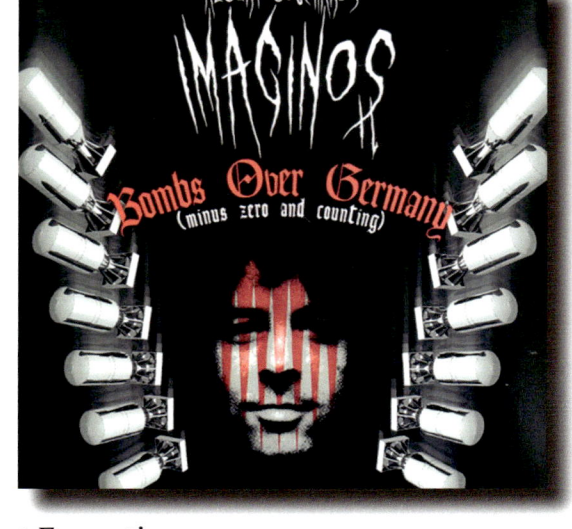

2022

June 3, 2022. Joe Bouchard issues a new album, called *American Rocker*.

2023

July 28, 2023. Albert Bouchard issues *Imaginos III: Mutant Formation*.

December 4, 2023. Albert Bouchard announces a graphic novel based on his first solo installment of the *Imaginos* saga.

December 8, 2023. Frontiers issues a two-CD/DVD BÖC live album called *50th Anniversary – Live in NYC – First Night*.

2024

February 7, 2024. Buck and Eric announce the end of Blue Öyster Cult's recording days, with an album of catalogue rarities re-constituted and re-recorded, called *Ghost Stories*.

Acknowledgements

As he's done with many of my books, the illustrious Agustin Garcia de Paredes deserves a mighty appreciation from us for his copy-edit of this book. Thanks to excellent BÖC site Hot Rails to Hull for their intense scholarship over the years. Thanks as well to the official band site and all those involved in the BÖC FAQ and other academic pursuits pursuant to the band, in particular Bolle Gregmar, John Swartz and Melne. This book is dedicated to our beloved Bolle Gregmar, fighting for a return to health and his rightful place documenting band lore.

Martin Popoff – A Complete Bibliography

2024: Honesty Is No Excuse: Thin Lizzy on Record, Van Halen at 50, Pictures at Eleven: Robert Plant Album by Album, Perfect Water: The Rebel Imaginos

2023: Kiss at 50, Dominance and Submission: The Blue Öyster Cult Canon, The Who and Quadrophenia, Wild Mood Swings: Disintegrating The Cure Album by Album, AC/DC at 50

2022: Pink Floyd and The Dark Side of the Moon: 50 Years, Killing the Dragon: Dio in the '90s and 2000s, Feed My Frankenstein: Alice Cooper, the Solo Years, Easy Action: The Original Alice Cooper Band, Lively Arts: The Damned Deconstructed, Yes: A Visual Biography II: 1982 – 2022, Bowie @ 75, Dream Evil: Dio in the '80s, Judas Priest: A Visual Biography, UFO: A Visual Biography

2021: Hawkwind: A Visual Biography, Loud 'n' Proud: Fifty Years of Nazareth, Yes: A Visual Biography, Uriah Heep: A Visual Biography, Driven: Rush in the '90s and "In the End," Flaming Telepaths: Imaginos Expanded and Specified, Rebel Rouser: A Sweet User Manual

2020: The Fortune: On the Rocks with Angel, Van Halen: A Visual Biography, Limelight: Rush in the '80s, Thin Lizzy: A Visual Biography, Empire of the Clouds: Iron Maiden in the 2000s, Blue Öyster Cult: A Visual Biography, Anthem: Rush in the '70s, Denim and Leather: Saxon's First Ten Years, Black Funeral: Into the Coven with Mercyful Fate

2019: Satisfaction: 10 Albums That Changed My Life, Holy Smoke: Iron Maiden in the '90s, Sensitive to Light: The Rainbow Story, Where Eagles Dare: Iron Maiden in the '80s, Aces High: The Top 250 Heavy Metal Songs of the '80s, Judas Priest: Turbo 'til Now, Born Again! Black Sabbath in the Eighties and Nineties

2018: Riff Raff: The Top 250 Heavy Metal Songs of the '70s, Lettin' Go: UFO in the '80s and '90s, Queen: Album by Album, Unchained: A Van Halen User Manual, Iron Maiden: Album by Album, Sabotage! Black Sabbath in the Seventies, Welcome to My Nightmare: 50 Years of Alice Cooper, Judas Priest: Decade of Domination, Popoff Archive – 6: American Power Metal, Popoff Archive – 5: European Power Metal, The Clash: All the Albums, All the Songs

2017: Led Zeppelin: All the Albums, All the Songs, AC/DC: Album by Album, Lights Out: Surviving the '70s with UFO, Tornado of Souls: Thrash's Titanic Clash, Caught in a Mosh: The Golden Era of Thrash, Rush: Album by Album, Beer Drinkers and Hell Raisers: The Rise of Motörhead, Metal Collector: Gathered Tales from Headbangers, Hit the Lights: The Birth of Thrash, Popoff Archive – 4: Classic Rock, Popoff Archive – 3: Hair Metal

2016: Popoff Archive – 2: Progressive Rock, Popoff Archive – 1: Doom Metal, Rock the Nation: Montrose, Gamma and Ronnie Redefined, Punk Tees: The Punk Revolution in 125 T-Shirts, Metal Heart: Aiming High with Accept, Ramones at 40, Time and a Word: The Yes Story

2015: Kickstart My Heart: A Mötley Crüe Day-by-Day, This Means War: The Sunset Years of the NWOBHM, Wheels of Steel: The Explosive Early Years of the NWOBHM, Swords and Tequila: Riot's Classic First Decade, Who Invented Heavy Metal?, Sail Away: Whitesnake's Fantastic Voyage

2014: Live Magnetic Air: The Unlikely Saga of the Superlative Max Webster, Steal Away the Night: An Ozzy Osbourne Day-by-Day, The Big Book of Hair Metal, Sweating Bullets: The Deth and Rebirth of Megadeth, Smokin' Valves: A Headbanger's Guide to 900 NWOBHM Records

2013: The Art of Metal (co-edit with Malcolm Dome), 2 Minutes to Midnight: An Iron Maiden Day-by-Day, Metallica: The Complete Illustrated History, Rush: The Illustrated History, Ye Olde Metal: 1979, Scorpions: Top of the Bill - updated and reissued as Wind of Change: The Scorpions Story in 2016

2012: Epic Ted Nugent, Fade To Black: Hard Rock Cover Art of the Vinyl Age, It's Getting Dangerous: Thin Lizzy 81-12, We Will Be Strong: Thin Lizzy 76-81, Fighting My Way Back: Thin Lizzy 69-76, The Deep Purple Royal Family: Chain of Events '80 – '11, The Deep Purple Royal Family: Chain of Events Through '79 - reissued as The Deep Purple Family Year by Year books

2011: Black Sabbath FAQ, The Collector's Guide to Heavy Metal: Volume 4: The '00s (co-authored with David Perri)

2010: Goldmine Standard Catalog of American Records 1948 – 1991, 7th Edition

2009: Goldmine Record Album Price Guide, 6th Edition, Goldmine 45 RPM Price Guide, 7th Edition, A Castle Full of Rascals: Deep Purple '83 – '09, Worlds Away: Voivod and the Art of Michel Langevin, Ye Olde Metal: 1978

2008: Gettin' Tighter: Deep Purple '68 – '76, All Access: The Art of the Backstage Pass, Ye Olde Metal: 1977, Ye Olde Metal: 1976

2007: Judas Priest: Heavy Metal Painkillers, Ye Olde Metal: 1973 to 1975, The Collector's Guide to Heavy Metal: Volume 3: The Nineties, Ye Olde Metal: 1968 to 1972

2006: Run for Cover: The Art of Derek Riggs, Black Sabbath: Doom Let Loose, Dio: Light Beyond the Black

2005: The Collector's Guide to Heavy Metal: Volume 2: The Eighties, Rainbow: English Castle Magic, UFO: Shoot Out the Lights, The New Wave of British Heavy Metal Singles

2004: Blue Öyster Cult: Secrets Revealed! – update and reissue 2009); updated and reissued as Agents of Fortune: The Blue Öyster Cult Story 2016, Contents Under Pressure: 30 Years of Rush at Home & Away, The Top 500 Heavy Metal Albums of All Time

2003: The Collector's Guide to Heavy Metal: Volume 1: The Seventies, The Top 500 Heavy Metal Songs of All Time

2001: Southern Rock Review

2000: Heavy Metal: 20th Century Rock and Roll, The Goldmine Price Guide to Heavy Metal Records

1997: The Collector's Guide to Heavy Metal

1993: Riff Kills Man! 25 Years of Recorded Hard Rock & Heavy Metal

See martinpopoff.com for complete details and ordering information.

About the Author

At approximately 7900 (with over 7000 appearing in his books), Martin has unofficially written more record reviews than anybody in the history of music writing across all genres. Additionally, Martin has penned approximately 120 books on hard rock, heavy metal, classic rock and record collecting. He was Editor-In-Chief of the now retired Brave Words & Bloody Knuckles, Canada's foremost metal publication for 14 years, and has also contributed to Revolver, Guitar World, Goldmine, Record Collector, bravewords.com, lollipop.com and hardradio.com, with many record label band bios and liner notes to his credit as well. Additionally, Martin has been a regular contractor to Banger Films, having worked for two years as researcher on the award-winning documentary *Rush: Beyond the Lighted Stage*, on the writing and research team for the 11-episode Metal Evolution and on the ten-episode Rock Icons, both for VH1 Classic. Additionally, Martin is the writer of the original metal genre chart used in *Metal: A Headbanger's Journey* and throughout the Metal Evolution episodes. Martin currently resides in Toronto and can be reached through martinp@inforamp.net or www.martinpopoff.com.